Raising Chickens
- For Eggs and Meat -

By
Mike Woolnough

Published by The Good Life Press Ltd. 2009

ISBN 978 1 90487 142 2
A catalogue record for this book is available from
the British Library.

Published by
The Good Life Press Ltd.
PO Box 536
Preston
PR2 9ZY

www.goodlifepress.co.uk
www.homefarmer.co.uk

Set by The Good Life Press Ltd.

Printed and bound in Great Britain on recycled paper
by The Cromwell Press Group, Trowbridge, Wiltshire

Raising Chickens
- For Eggs and Meat -

By

Mike Woolnough

The Good Life Press LTD

Contents

Foreword | 7

Chapter 1 | 9 - 32
Getting Started

Chapter 2 | 33 - 42
The Breeds

Chapter 3 | 43 - 65
Housing

Chapter 4 | 66 - 75
Feeding

Chapter 5 | 76 - 115
Breeding

Chapter 6l | 116 - 120
Culling

Chapter 7 | 121 - 130
Oven Ready

Chapter 8 | 131 - 147
Problems

Chapter 9| 148 - 156
In the Kitchen

Resources | 157 - 160

Foreword

So you watched all the episodes of Hugh's Chicken Run and felt quite guilty, followed by a helping of Jamie's Fowl Dinners – or should that have been Foul Dinners – and you are now quite nauseated at the thought of how your food is produced, and would like to raise your own ethically-produced eggs and/or meat.....

Great! You have taken the first step by making that choice, but now you have to decide just how far you want to take it. Do you just want a couple of hens to give you fresh eggs for your breakfast, or would you like to have a roast chicken that has more flavour than anything you can buy in the shops?

Fifty years ago chicken was a luxury, normally eaten only at Christmas or on special occasions and many a family raised their own chickens in the backyard. A turkey at Christmas was practically unheard of. The growth of the modern chicken mass production system has brought the price of a chicken down to a pittance, but at the expense of taste. The tasteless cardboard chicken sold in supermarkets bears no comparison to home grown.

Completely sickened by the battery factories we have been successfully raising chickens for both eggs and meat for the past 10 years on our allotment. We do not pretend to be experts but we hope that our book is an introduction for anyone, who like us, wants to raise a few chickens and provide for their family.

Michael Woolnough
Suffolk, 2009

Chapter One
Getting Started

In the same way that there is a world of difference between a Lamborghini and a Morris Minor, so there are poultry that have been bred over hundreds of years to produce lots of eggs but don't put on an ounce of spare meat, and some that grow huge but don't lay many eggs. In the middle are what are called utility birds, which lay quite a lot of eggs and are a decent size for a meal. These are the traditional breeds that have been kept on farmyards and smallholdings for many years and have stood the test of time.

In addition to the traditional breeds, recent years have seen a large number of hybrids appearing on the scene, many of them having been developed from the commercial battery hen breeds. They will lay an egg nearly every day for around two years, and then virtually stop. The factory farms generally slaughter them after eighteen months and bring in new birds, as they don't want to feed them through their annual moult when they don't lay at all. The slaughtered birds are generally shredded to be processed into soups and similar products as they carry little meat.

So, there is a bewildering choice of birds available to you – or is there? This book is not aimed at "chicken-fanciers" who love all the weird and wonderful breeds…yes there really is something called a Transylvanian Naked Neck for instance….neither is it a comprehensive guide to chicken-keeping. The idea is to give you a helping hand towards making a start with keeping chickens that will help to pay for their keep by giving you wonderfully tasty meals, probably as part of a bigger plan of self-sufficiency, and steering you clear of some of the worst pitfalls.

Don't go into your new enterprise thinking that you can make money from it, or produce eggs or your Sunday roast on the cheap – it doesn't work that way. The commercial operations purchase everything in bulk to keep down costs, and you will be raising your meat birds for six months instead of less than six weeks as they do. There are also very strict laws regarding the sale of eggs and meat that change regularly, not to mention the fact that your local tax inspector will be very interested if he hears that you are selling your products.

Your eggs will have superb deep orange yolks though, that were produced by the wonderful range of natural foods that you have given to your hens, instead of by artificial colouring in their feed, and the firm tender meat will make your mouth water whilst giving you a clear conscience that it was not produced at the expense of terrible suffering to the bird.

You also have to be aware that you are taking on a big commitment. Chickens are not like a dog or cat – you can't take them away on holiday with you, and there is no such thing as poultry kennels.

You will need friends or family willing to collect eggs and check feed and water when you are away. Whilst you can cover the situation for a few days by using several feeders and drinkers, it is not recommended....and you are likely to return to find your nest boxes full of hens sitting on the eggs that have been uncollected.

We have left a hen happily sitting on eggs in a coop in the garden unattended for a week, but we always make arrangements for our main flocks to be supervised.

Having gotten this far, and decided that you are still interested in keeping some chickens, the first elementary decision that you have to take is whether you are hoping for just eggs, or eggs and meat. If you want to raise your own meat, then this generally means that you will have to hatch your own chicks. By and large, you will hatch equal numbers of males and females, and will be raising both to maturity. There is a way of producing sex-linked chicks in some breeds, whereby the male chicks are one colour, and the female chicks another. This is how the commercial boys breed their poultry. One of the most damning pieces of information that came from the Jamie Oliver TV programmes was that Britain raises 855 million chickens each year for meat, and that all of them are female. This means that 855 million males are killed at one day old, many of them shredded alive, and their lives have been wasted. I couldn't breed my stock that way, and as you are reading a book dedicated to ethical methods, I can't see that you the reader would want to either.

Therefore, you have to consider if you can raise cockerels in your location. They are noisy, believe me they are noisy! The young lads will certainly be crowing by 12 weeks old, and it could be much younger. You will be keeping them until they are around 26 weeks old, provided that your neighbours haven't anonymously poisoned them in the meantime, or, more likely, complained to the local council public nuisance department. The popular fallacy is that a cockerel will crow at dawn – cockcrow – but in fact they can do it at any time of day or night…..and remember that in any case dawn is very early during the summer months.

Ask yourself, quite honestly, if you can keep cockerels. If the answer is "no", then you should be looking at producing eggs only, and your hens won't need a boy around to achieve that for you. Some people claim that hens like to have a cockerel around, but in our experience this isn't true and they will live

All cockerels crow, there are no exceptions. Here a magnificent Golden Cuckoo Marans is lustily exercising his lungs.

quite happily without a bothersome boy around the place.

If you have access to a good supply of fertile eggs of your chosen breed, then it is possible to raise young without the need to feed a rooster all the year round to produce them, and cut down on the noise factor. Any male young will of course crow, but it will only be until they reach oven-ready size, then peace and quiet will be resumed.

Alternatively, you could purchase day-old or young stock from a breeder, and choose a variety that has sex-linked colouring, purchasing only females.

Having made your decision, you now have to look at how much space you have available. I will go into housing in some detail later in the book, but it does have a bearing on which breed of chicken you choose. There are many chicken coops on the market that really aren't suitable for housing large birds on a permanent basis unless moved every two or three days to a new patch of ground.

Do you intend to keep your poultry at home, or do you plan on keeping them on local allotments, as we do? If you already have an allotment, and there are other chickens on the field, then getting permission from the Council to keep your own birds there shouldn't be a problem.

If you are new to allotmenteering then a word of caution is in order.

Don't ring the secretary up and ask him for an allotment as you want to keep chickens. Many officials have a built-in aversion to livestock, fearing that it will cause them more paperwork and problems. It is better to ask for a plot to grow vegetables, get established, and then apply for permission for chooks. Don't expect to be allowed to build your run on part of the plot and let the rest of it grow wild either – you will be expected to keep it neat, tidy and cultivated. Failure to do so will get you served with an eviction notice. Similarly, most secretaries will not be happy if you turn your entire plot into one enormous chicken run. Allotments are intended as a place to grow fruit and vegetables – livestock is tolerated in moderation.

Not all councils allow chickens to be kept on allotments, and very few of them will tolerate cockerels at all. You may be able to get away with slipping one on for breeding purposes and then very quickly shipping him out again before anybody has a chance to complain, but don't count on it, and certainly don't plan on housing a boy on your plot long term.

Similarly, some property deeds, particularly on newly built houses, may prohibit the keeping of chickens or indeed any animals on your property. Some local councils require planning permission for any outhouses or sheds, and you should check all these restrictions before building a large chicken house and run in your garden.

Choosing your breed

Chickens come in two sizes, large fowl and bantams. Bantams are generally scaled-down versions of the larger breeds, although there are a few bantams, known as true bantams, for which no large type exists. These true bantams originated from the island of Java, and were shipped out through a port called Banten which was Anglicized to Bantam, hence their name. Bantam has since been applied to anything small and pugnacious, including bantamweight boxers. During the First World War, when increasingly large numbers of troops were needed, the height requirement for recruits was lowered, and thousands of shorter men joined up together, giving rise to their name – the Bantam Battalions.

Seabrights are one of the best known breeds of true bantam. Bantam breeds have been the mainstay of local poultry shows for many years, often accounting for two thirds of the show entry. This is due to their convenient size, and this is also handy for those of us who are limited for choice because of space restrictions. Bantams can be raised for the table, but they are not going to feed eight people for a Sunday roast, as a large fowl can. They do eat considerably less than large fowl, however, and require less space for housing and runs. You have to bear in mind that their eggs are substantially smaller - three of the largest bantam eggs are around the quantity of two large fowl eggs. True bantams, which are way too small for our purposes, are totally unsuitable, but bantam versions of breeds such as Sussex, Wyandotte, Rhode Island Red, Welsummer or Indian Game will all prove useful for those of you that don't have the room for large fowl.

This photograph, which shows the difference in size between a Light Sussex large fowl and a bantam, was taken on a dark and dreary November morning. Even though it is black and white, you can clearly see that the bantam has finished her moult and is coming back into lay as her comb is dark and healthy and her plumage is immaculate.

The large fowl, by comparison, has a pale and listless comb. She appears to have moulted her body feathers, but the tail is yet to be dropped and regrown

A bantam should be one quarter of the weight of its large fowl cousin.

Don't think that you can avoid the problem of noisy cockerels by keeping bantams though. True, they don't have a deep crow that carries a long way like large fowl, but my experience is that they crow twice as often and it is more of a high-pitched shriek! They are also considerably more aggressive than most of their large fowl distant cousins, and will think nothing of instantly attacking a bird five or six times their size – and usually winning the ensuing fight.

Bantams are also usually considerably more "flighty" – this means that if startled they will take to the skies. A six foot fence is no barrier to a bantam, and runs need to be wired over to prevent escapes. Once out and three gardens away they are extremely difficult to recapture, believe me – we've been there!

I won't be going into details of soft or hard feather varieties, or breed/show standards – why complicate things when you just want some tasty eggs and want to know how to go about it? There are many very comprehensive chicken encyclopaedias on the market that will give you every fact and figure that you could possibly want, provided that you don't fall asleep in the meantime from boredom. But this book is aimed at people who are considering keeping some chickens as part of a programme of self-sufficiency.

Egg Birds

As previously mentioned, if you want an egg from each hen virtually every day you could plump for one of the commercial hybrids such as a Lohmann or Warren. After two years their laying is likely to tail off dramatically though and you will have to decide what to do with them. Are you prepared to treat them as pets and pay for their feed and get very little in return? Or would you be hard-hearted enough to dispose of them in some way, even though the hens will have virtually no meat on them.

It's a dilemma, isn't it?

There are hundreds of people throughout the UK rescuing

battery hens and giving them a good home for the rest of their natural lives. The Battery Hen Welfare Trust organises rescue runs whereby they find new homes for thousands of birds at a time when a battery unit decides that the birds have outlived their usefulness. If you are happy to get a few eggs each week on an ongoing but reducing scale then perhaps you should contact the BHWT and ask about availability.

You should be prepared for a shock when you get your birds though as they are likely to be in a terrible state, with many feathers missing and pecking injuries, possibly clipped beaks, and looking sorry for themselves. They won't recognise anything as food except the pellets or mash that they are used to, won't know how to roost, and will be scared of the great outdoors. Remember that they have spent their short lives cramped in tiny pens.

Having said all this, they soon recover and re-grow their plumage, and can develop wonderful characters. You shouldn't keep them with non-battery hens though as there is a risk that they will carry diseases. Battery hens are often vaccinated, and drip-fed antibiotics daily to prevent diseases spreading through the many thousands of tightly-packed birds. Whilst they might not develop a full-blown illness it is quite possible that they may still be a carrier, and affect your unvaccinated birds.

However, if you are serious about your egg production, the best solution is probably to plump for one of the traditional egg breeds such as Leghorns which will lay quite large numbers of eggs that gradually decline over three or four years, and will still lay some eggs after that. Don't forget that chickens can live a long time, although around six years is average. If you choose to breed from your stock to provide your own replacement hens, you will still have to decide what to do with your cockerels. The cock birds of egg laying breeds will have a reasonable amount of meat on them, unlike the hens, whose protein all goes into egg production.

One (in my opinion) minor point to consider is the colour of the eggs that your chosen breed will produce. No, I don't mean the colour of the yolk, I'm talking about the shell colour. Personally, the shell colour doesn't make any difference to me, and it certainly doesn't affect the taste of the contents, but the British do seem to prefer a light brown egg, whilst the Americans prefer white. The current fashion craze is blue eggs, which I must admit are rather attractive. Colours range from the dark chocolate brown of Marans and Welsummers, through the light brown/buff of Sussex, the green of Legbars, the blue of Araucanas to the white of Leghorns. If you are interested only in egg production, then perhaps a mix of breeds to provide a multicoloured selection for your eggboxes may be the answer for you.

Meat birds

Again, there are many hybrids available these days as a result of breeding for fast growth. Sasso chickens are probably the best known. They are ready for killing at five to six weeks, but grow so fast that their legs can't take their weight and are often malformed and bent. If you want to keep your own breeding stock you literally have to half starve them to keep them slim enough to be capable of mating or laying eggs. I'm sure that this is really not how you envisaged raising chickens. There are, however, some traditional breeds that will produce a good-sized carcass at around the twenty week stage onwards. They gain this size at the expense of egg laying capacity, however, and the adults will produce a lot less eggs per year than the egg birds mentioned above. If you are interested in raising good big birds, and aren't worried about large numbers of eggs, then perhaps you should consider Brahmas or Cochins. Cockerels of these breeds can reach up to thirteen pounds in weight. They need a little more care than some other breeds as they have very feathery feet, and so can't cope with wet, muddy conditions very well, but they are well worth the effort, and are very gentle giants.

Utility birds

The traditional meat breeds, before man began messing about with blood lines commercially, were the Light Sussex, and the Dorking. Curiously there were strains of these breeds that were also excellent layers. As the commercial strains of hybrids have developed these traditional breeds have fallen by the wayside and are not seen in the big chicken units......
didn't they have a lucky escape?

Luckily their worth has been appreciated by backyard enthusiasts and smallholders and many of the bloodlines have remained pure.

Some of the other breeds that make good utility birds are Rhode Island Reds, Orpingtons, Welsummers, New Hampshire Reds, Wyandottes and Indian Game. One of the best meat birds is reputedly a Dorking crossed with an Indian Game.

In this case you would eat both the males and females as crossbreeds should not be sold for breeding. It is important to keep the traditional breeds pure. Indian Game have yellow skin, which doesn't look particularly appealing to some people.

There is no reason why you shouldn't go for a mix of colours to have an attractive looking flock to brighten up your

The Orpington is one breed that has suffered particularly badly in the utility stakes in the search for the perfect show bird. The offspring of this beautiful White Orpington cock will lay far fewer eggs than their ancestors of 100 years ago, and he bears little resemblance to his forefathers. Photo: Julie & Dean Short

garden, but you should be aware that some of the colours have been obtained at the cost of size or egg production. For instance Sussex chickens have mostly kept their size in most colours, but the Coronation variety is often smaller. We love their beautiful dove grey colouring, and by mating our Coronations with a big Light Sussex boy we have managed to build up the size of following generations.

Certainly a flock of Light, Buff, Coronation and Red Sussex is a wonderful sight.....and there are also Brown, Silver and Speckled varieties.

I have already mentioned that there are ways to breed chickens that produce sex-linked colours, but dismissed it because the normal way to use this method is to kill the males at birth. There is an area where this characteristic can be useful, however. Later I will talk about the ways of sexing your youngsters, but they are not reliable by any means, and if you intend to sell your female offspring this can be a problem.

The way to get round it is to mate a cockerel with the red gene to a hen carrying the silver gene. I'm not going to go into the genetics of chickens, because there have been whole books written on the subject and it is very complicated, and quite honestly I don't understand very much about it myself. I do know, however, that if you mate a male Buff Sussex (gold gene) with a hen Light Sussex (silver gene) all the female chicks will be a dusty golden colour and will grow into pure Buff Sussex that you can sell at any age with confidence, and all the yellow chicks will grow into Light Sussex boys that you can grow to maturity for the table. The boys must not be sold or used for breeding as they are impure and carry the gold gene – this can be seen as they grow by a yellow sheen across their backs.

There are red and silver gene carrying colours in most of the utility breeds of birds, and so this method can almost certainly be used if you prefer to breed a different variety such as Dorking or Wyandotte, but you must investigate first to ensure that the female young will be pure stock rather than crossbreeds.

Alternatively, you could go for Legbars. The chicks of this breed can be sexed at birth by the barring on their backs and they produce a reasonable meat bird – and lay the most gorgeous blue eggs.

You should avoid buying your stock from a keeper who breeds their chickens for showing. They will keep their best birds for the show table or their breeding programme, and sell off their slightly substandard birds. Don't get me wrong, there is nothing wrong with this if you are just looking for some birds that will give you some eggs and look good in your garden. However, show birds are generally somewhat inbred to retain or improve the good showing points, and often egg laying quantities and fertility are affected. The feather quality of show birds can also be adversely affected by inbreeding, resulting in a mass of soft, fluffy growth that can make mating difficult. Show quality hens often have to have the feathers trimmed away from their vent to be able to mate successfully. A classic example of this is the Orpington, which has been bred for show purposes to resemble a huge feather duster, and egg-laying has suffered as a result. A chicken only has so much protein that it can absorb and use constructively – and it's a choice between feathers or meat.

I suppose that I must at this stage confess to being terribly biased, as I have had a long love affair with Sussex chickens. When I first mooted the subject of keeping some hens my wife borrowed every chookbook from the local library and after reading them all cover to cover she announced that she wouldn't mind some Light Sussex as they seemed to have a nice nature! We began with a pair of them in the garden, and have kept them ever since, even though we tried other breeds. We have raised all the different colour varieties in large fowl and bantams, and have found them all to be lovely, reliable birds.

They produce good sized table birds, lay plenty of eggs, and are universally popular so you never have any difficulty selling any spare pullets. They are extremely good sitters too. In fact the bantams can be too good and will even try to incubate a gold ball placed in their nestbox!

To be fair, the other breeds mentioned above such as Dorking or Wyandotte would probably serve you just as well – although Rhode Island Reds rarely sit well and Welsummers nearly always have to be incubated. However, when you consider all the relevant factors; egg laying, meat production, character, hardiness, colour varieties, and sitting ability, we personally feel that nothing beats the Sussex.

How many?

How many chickens should I buy? That is the sixty four thousand dollar question. Any given group of chickens will always have an established pecking order, with a 'Top Hen' who is prepared to take on all comers to defend her title. New birds introduced into such a flock will get a severe battering from all the hens in the flock, all defending their own place in the hierarchy. For this reason many books argue that even if you only want a couple of hens, always, if possible, plan for at least three birds so that if one dies you are still left with two that will keep each other company. Chickens are social flock animals, and one kept on its own will just pine and mope around. The theory, however, is that if you try to introduce a replacement, then world war three will break out.

I don't fully agree with this, as there is always a good chance that, at some time in the future, you will want to add extra birds. Chickens are very addictive and there will always be the "We can squeeze in just one more" syndrome. You will always face this dilemma anyway when returning a bird to the flock that has been brooding and raising chicks and has therefore been away for a while. There is a simple solution providing that you have enough housing available: cage the lone hen with another bird from the flock – preferably the Top Hen – in a new cage. They are therefore then both newcomers and will settle down after a little bickering. If need be you can then put the pair of them into a new run and add two more from the flock. The buddy system means that the two pairs will defend their new-found partners, and equal numbers of 'old gang' and 'new gang' are what you are always looking for as an ideal way of adding new birds. This soon becomes one new gang, and can be re-introduced to the original flock with a lot less fighting, or one bird being badly victimised. Chickens aren't actually very nice birds at all and will have no compunction in pecking a bullied bird to death.

You also have to ask yourself just how many eggs you can eat. You may think that if you have lovely fresh eggs you will eat more, and to an extent this is true, but the novelty does wear off. Work out how many eggs you eat as a family now, including those used in baking etc., and add perhaps fifty percent to allow for increased consumption and storing some to use later in the year when the birds are moulting and not laying. If you calculate at the rate of three eggs daily from four hens you probably won't be too far off the mark. Plus, of course, any you may plan to give away.

You will see that you actually don't need many hens to satisfy your needs. Four to six are usually more than enough for the average family. Don't be tempted to keep more to sell excess eggs – it really isn't economic to do so.

You also should not overcrowd your birds in housing that is too small for the number of chooks you keep. There are certain serious illnesses (more details later) that lie dormant within poultry, but can be triggered into activity by the stress of overcrowding.....and in any case we are aiming to keep our birds in good conditions, not like battery hens.

Don't expect eggs straight away the first morning after you have bought your hens. Birds are generally sold at what is called point of lay (POL), which is a bit misleading as this can mean anything from 12 weeks onwards, when in fact they often don't start laying until they are around 26 weeks. Under 12 weeks it takes a really experienced person to be able to sex most breeds with any great accuracy. When buying make sure that you can swap any birds that suddenly decide that they are not going to start laying but rather fancy crowing instead. Young cockerels that are in with older, stronger boys will try not to attract the attention of the 'top dog' for fear of a beating, and so will keep a very low profile and seldom crow and sometimes even fail to grow a comb and wattles. Take them away from that threatening situation and they will soon start exercising their lungs.

If you are intending to breed your own birds, then you obviously need a cockerel too, or those poor hens are going to sit on those eggs for a very long time to no avail and feel very frustrated. Although your six hens can all be sisters, the cockerel should be unrelated, or you will be inbreeding, which as already mentioned isn't a good thing. It's always best to get all your hens from the same person, and even from the same run, as they will already have an established pecking order and won't set out to kill each other the second they are released into their new run when you get them home. It is, however, a good idea to get your lad from a different breeder altogether. There will be no domination fights like there are amongst hens – the cock will show them who is boss very quickly and that will be that! He should be at least as old as the hens though, and preferably a little older, or like all men he will very quickly be henpecked. It is best if the hens are not yet laying when he is introduced, as it will produce a much quieter settling in period.

If they are laying then the hen pen will resemble a Roman orgy as he will try to mate with everything in sight!

Some breeders will only sell their chickens in trios – a cock and two hens. This is a way for them to solve the cockerel problem as they are probably breeding far too many birds to be able to spare the time, space and feed to raise all that they produce to table weight. These trios are almost always from the same brood and so will at the very least be half-brothers and sisters, and should be avoided. Only if the breeder is running two completely separate bloodlines (which is rare) should you consider a trio.

If at all possible buy your stock from somebody that has been recommended to you. It is usually fairly easy to find somebody locally that keeps chickens and they can point you towards a reputable breeder. There are also forums on the internet, poultry magazines, and local poultry clubs that could all give you advice.

Don't be tempted to buy from markets as, apart from specialist rare breeds sales, they are often dumping grounds for unsaleable stock, and the sellers will generally know a lot more than you do. We bought eight six week old Buff Sussex chicks 'as hatched' from a local auction. Six weeks later all eight of them started crowing – the seller obviously knew how to sex them at an early age. We learned this skill ourselves after a couple of years.....sexing young chicks that is, not dumping males in markets.

Poultry markets are also likely to be hotbeds of illness, as the cramped stressed conditions, and close proximity of pens are ideal conditions for the spread of disease.

If you can't get all the hens that you want from one breeder, or are forced to buy from a market, then great care has to be taken when you get them home. Apart from fighting, there is a very real danger of disease and cross-infection. Each group of birds will have developed immunity to the bugs that it has come into contact with, or may still be in the incubation stage. Stick them in with other birds and you could have an epidemic on your hands. Similarly you should never put vaccinated birds in with unvaccinated ones – although they can't get the disease themselves they may well be a carrier and could immediately infect the unvaccinated ones.

If you are aiming to breed from your birds straight away, then it is better to try to find adult birds. Hens (2nd year+) generally lay bigger eggs than pullets (first year birds) and these are much better for hatching as they give the chick more room to move round when it is trying to break its way out of the egg, and will contain more sustenance for the growing youngsters through a larger yolk.

Do keep any new birds in isolation for at least a couple of weeks to make sure that all is well. Sadly we didn't, which proved to be a very big mistake!

We bought two Light Sussex pullets (the term for young hens before they have been through their first moult) from a big local poultry dealership. We were puzzled that the lady caught one, held it to her ear, then put it down again and caught two others. When we asked her about this she said that it was "a little chesty". We were too green to realise that we should have walked away there and then, and she was too afraid of losing her sale – we were buying a big henhouse, feeders, and all the other paraphernalia that a beginner needs – that she knowingly sold us birds that had been with a sick one.

One of these birds didn't grow, sat around and moped all day (we actually named her Moaning Myrtle). She just wasted away to a bag of bones, and eventually I had to put her out of her misery. Her partner was very runty but survived, so we went looking for a replacement.....or three as it turned out.

By this time we had found a wonderful man near us who loved his birds and bred beautiful, healthy stock. We bought three lovely pullets and took them home – and they were all sick within a week of coming into contact with our puny survivor.

This had us beating a path to the vet's surgery and resulted in my having to give them all injections every morning and night for ten days – an experience I wouldn't wish on any of you. The medicine cost nearly as much as the birds did too!

Being extremely slow learners we did the same thing again a few months later, with the same outcome. The new birds didn't seem unhealthy, but chickens can carry some diseases without visible signs. When they become stressed or tired then the illness can assert itself.

This time one of the birds that we had to give injections to was Hagrid, our huge Light Sussex rooster. This involved snatching him off his perch in the dark (incidentally, the easiest way to catch chickens), bringing him indoors and standing him on our dining room table, with my wife hanging onto him while I stuck the needle in his chest. Bearing in mind that Sue doesn't like things that flutter, and Hagrid was a big old boy, she was very brave. All went well until one evening when I must have hit a nerve with the needle, and he went ballistic, thrashing around with a hypodermic hanging out of his chest! To her credit, Sue managed to hang onto him, and he was none the worse for his shock.

After this we very rarely bought in new stock as live birds, but preferred to buy fertile eggs of the given breed and hatch them ourselves. This is something you could do yourself to get your initial stock, but you would have to remember that a percentage won't hatch, at least half are likely to be boys, and you will have to wait at least six months for eggs.

Examine your potential new purchases carefully. Don't be afraid to handle them and take a close look. Check the feathers around their vents – if these are fouled then it is a sure sign that the bird has loose droppings, often one of the first signs of something more serious. The bird should feel reasonably plump and certainly not be all skin and bone, and should have bright and alert eyes. Discharge from nostrils or beak is not acceptable, and if you can feel or hear a rattle in its chest when it breathes, then this is a big NO.

If your journey isn't too long the best way to transport you purchases home is in cardboard boxes just a little bit bigger than the birds. Although this may seem a little cruel in fact it isn't as the birds will settle down in the dark and not get stressed. They don't need food or water unless your journey will be more than two hours, in which case something like a cat or dog carrier would probably be more suitable as it would be better ventilated and the birds can see to eat and drink.

Depending on what type of housing you have purchased, it is a good idea to keep your new chooks shut in the house section for a couple of days, provided that it is big enough. This way they will learn where home is and return to it for roosting. Having their feeders inside the house will help too.

If the house isn't big enough and you have to let the new birds into the run straight away, be prepared to have fun at dusk getting them back indoors. Chickens really are not the brightest of creatures and will sleep sitting on the floor in the rain rather than enter a strange dark house. We developed our own method for getting new acquisitions into shelter at night after a large Light Sussex nearly broke our kitchen window after being attracted to the lit (but closed!) window – we now place a lit torch inside the bedroom section of their housing just before dusk and the birds go in quite happily, following the light. After a couple of days there is no need to do it as they have learned where to go. If you intend to let your chickens free range in your garden then let them get settled into the house and run for a few days, and the first time you let them out, do so half an hour before they normally roost. Anything longer than half an hour, and they can't remember how to get back. Again, after a couple of days habit sets in and there are no further problems.

Be warned that they will trash your garden, scratch up all the grass and eat almost anything that grows. We were plagued with lily beetle before we got chickens, but they soon ate all the eggs or grubs and we weren't troubled any more. We didn't have any lilies either though, as the chickens had eaten them when all the new growth appeared.

Chickens also like to gather on your back door step so that they can greet you when you appear with some goodies for them. The downside is that they leave you presents all over your step that squelch when you step out in bare feet.
Don't forget that chickens are birds and can fly. Large fowl will rarely get over anything over four feet high unless very scared (or hungry, but bantams can get over a six foot high fence with ease. We had to wait for darkness to descend so that we could catch an escapee bantam roosting on our neighbours greenhouse roof once, rescuing her from

Nothing in your garden will be safe if you free range your chickens. If you want to keep at least part of your garden looking nice then wire off a section and allow the birds to do their worst there. Alternatively, just let them out for an hour or so each day.

the circling tomcats in the process. The way to stop your bantams from forming an Escape Committee is to clip the flight feathers on one wing only, as this destabilises them. Don't forget that the feathers grow again and you will need to re-clip them periodically.

You also have to keep an eye on them in case they dig an escape tunnel. I kid you not; their scratching-around excavations can take them under fences as well as over them.

Having mentioned the local cats, I should say that generally they aren't a problem. We heard a hell of a racket in our shrub bed one day, and a large tabby came charging out of the undergrowth and sped off up the garden, hotly pursued by our flock. It never came into the garden again. I think the

Clip one wing of each bird to prevent them fleeing the coop. Be careful not to cut the feathers too short, as they will bleed if you do so. Look closely and you will see that the quill near the root is dark, and becomes lighter further along. Cut one inch away from the dark area to be safe.

cats were braver with our escapee as the bantam was clearly distressed and looking for a roost. We kept chickens of all sizes, including small chicks, loose in the garden, and never lost one.

Even a visiting sparrowhawk left them alone. The same cannot be said of dogs, and we know several people that have lost their precious birds to marauding canines. Your own dog can usually be persuaded to leave them alone, but you have to protect them from outsiders. Our back gate still has a 'Think Chicken!' sign on it to make sure that the gate is always closed.

Chapter Two
The Breeds

Whilst I have already stated that this book isn't intended to be a chicken encyclopaedia, I do feel that a few of the most well known breeds should be described in a little detail to help you decide on the type that you would like.

Araucana

WOW, those beautiful blue eggs! Unfortunately many of the birds now sold no longer lay the beautiful pale blue eggs as their bloodlines have been contaminated by indiscriminate breeding, so be careful of what you buy. Egg-laying performance has also been badly hit, and you will be lucky to get 160 eggs a year from a good strain now, when well over 200 was a regular figure sixty years ago.

This rather comical looking bird has a beard and muffs that make them look rather like Uncle Albert from "Only Fools and Horses".

Although brought to Europe from South America, there is now scientific evidence that the original stock was brought to Peru by Polynesian voyagers long before, suggesting that the breed originated in Asia, the area that so many fowl can regard as their cradle.

The cock can reach seven pounds in weight, making them a reasonable meat breed.

Brahma

This breed takes its name from the Brahmaputra river in India, an indication of where its roots may lie, although there is now some doubt about this. A big bird, it can reach twelve pounds, but is slow developing and so youngish birds killed for meat will weigh substantially less. Like most breeds its egg-laying performance has been damaged by show breeders, and it can only be considered a moderate layer.

Don't let its large size and appearance deter you from keeping this breed as it is a true gentle giant – to the point of being rather a wimp! However, due to its size it doesn't always make a good sitter, so other hatching methods may have to be used.

Feathered feet mean that this breed needs similar treatment to Cochins.

Cochin

Even bigger than the Brahma, Cochins are the heavyweights of the chicken world, sometimes reaching over twelve pounds in weight. Inbreeding for show purposes has led to a proliferation of fluffy feathers and a decrease in egg production, which is a shame. Due to their feathered legs and feet Cochins should not be free-ranged, but where possible kept in good sized covered pens, ensuring that litter is kept dry. Perches should be kept low, and they should not be overfed as they are not active birds, and will run to fat. Again, its great size belies a very gentle nature.

Feathers around the vent region will almost certainly have to be clipped in both sexes in order to achieve successful mating.

Cochins are not as clumsy as Brahmas, and a sitting hen is less likely to break her eggs, although you may have to wait for her third year before she becomes broody.

Dorking

The Dorking, or something very similar to it, is widely believed to have been the first chicken to arrive in the British Isles, brought here by the Romans. The Dorking is unique in that it has five toes, whereas other breeds have only four. It is quite an active breed, which needs plenty of space. A wonderful meat bird, reaching weights of up to fourteen pounds or so, it is a reasonably good layer. There can be problems with them raising their own chicks, so using a bantam foster mother or an incubator may be necessary. They are quite gentle birds, but the variety of colours available is a little limited.

Indian Game

Although arguably the best pure breed meat chicken, the Indian game is one tough cookie! You only have to take one look at their stocky, muscular body and thickset legs to see that they are a bit of a bruiser. They can be quite aggressive towards both their own breed  and others, can have problems mating and don't produce many eggs. They are definitely not a suitable breed for the inexperienced!

Indian game cocks only reach eight pounds in weight, but crossing them with a Sussex or Dorking produces a superb table bird.

Ixworth

I couldn't write a book about utility poultry breeding without mentioning my local bird. The Ixworth is named after a village here in my home county of Suffolk, where it was created, and was intended to counter the new dual purpose birds coming out of America in the 1930s. It is extremely rare these days, and there are very few distinct bloodlines in existence. It is a useful bird, but is best kept under free range conditions as it doesn't do well when confined, and is probably best left to the experienced poultry keeper.

Jersey Giant

The biggest of the big, this huge bird has never really caught on with either domestic or commercial breeders. It is a little surprising bearing in mind that it is a good meat bird, with roosters usually reaching thirteen pounds, and the hens are also reasonably prolific layers.

It may be because black birds aren't particularly popular – certainly we didn't like the Silver Sussex and only kept them for a while – but there are also White and Blue versions available, both of which are attractive. More active than the other large breeds, unlike them it doesn't have feathered feet with their associated problems, and is also docile. I once knew somebody with a Jersey Giant that spent almost as much time with him in his kitchen as it did in the garden!

Leghorn

Probably one of the best-known egglaying chickens, and used in the production of many other breeds including the Rhode Island Red, the Leghorn originates from that home of the great egg layers, the Mediterranean area. Probably named after the Italian port of

Livorno known in English as Leghorn, the huge erect comb of the Leghorn cock is unmistakeable, whilst that of the female flops across one eye, and looks like a red beret.

This breed is notoriously flighty, and a covered run is pretty much essential. They are also very noisy, with the rooster crowing long and often, so consideration should be given to neighbours. Don't even think about trying to get a Leghorn hen to sit – I think they forgot how to about a century ago!

Legbar

The Cream Legbar is the result of the crossing of a Brown Leghorn with a Barred Rock, with a bit of Araucana thrown in to introduce the blue egg gene. Leghorns produce white eggs, and the blue gene dominates this, but there are some strains of Cream Legbar that produce olive coloured eggs because a buff egg layer has been introduced into the mix somewhere in the past. If you want blue eggs, make sure that you check with the breeder that these are what you will get. The current craze for blue eggs has led to some rather unscrupulous breeding, and pure Legbars are rather hard to find these days, and there are many weird and wonderful crossbreeds being sold as legbars. Care should particularly be exercised when buying hatching eggs or you may get an unpleasant surprise six months down the line when your hatchlings begin laying.

Cream Legbars also have some fertility problems resulting in poor hatch rates.

This is an autosexing breed, meaning that the chicks can be sexed on hatching due to colour differences. Cream Legbars can be regarded as utility birds as the Barred Rock part of their heritage means that they produce a reasonable sized carcass.

There are also Gold and Silver Legbars, with a slightly different lineage that does not include the Araucana, and so they lay white eggs.

Similar crossing experiments produced other sex-linked breeds such as the Welbar (Welsummer-Barred Rock) and Rhodebar (Rhode Island-Red-Barred Rock) and many others, most of which have now fallen by the wayside or become very rare. The Cream Legbar is by far and away the most popular sex-linked breed.

Marans

A common mistake with this chicken is to call a single bird a Maran, which is incorrect – Marans is the breed name, taken from the French village where it originated. A very good utility bird, which lays dark brown eggs provided you buy your stock from a good strain, care has to be taken if housing Marans with other breeds as they can be aggressive and bullying. This can also apply to their attitude to their keepers!

They are extremely good birds for free-ranging and are generally hardy and trouble free. The Cuckoo variety, with its distinctive mottled plumage and bold stance, is perhaps one of the most readily-identified breeds, and you can reasonably expect 200+ eggs a year.

New Hampshire Red

The large fowl are much harder to find than the bantams. They have the appearance of the traditional farmyard brown hen, but in fact they only arrived in the UK in the mid-1930s. The perfect utility bird, albeit with much-reduced egg laying capabilities than in their heyday, I wouldn't recommend free-ranging them around young children as the roosters can be somewhat aggressive and an older cock with big spurs can cause injury. Similarly, keeping more than one cock bird together can create problems. Hens are extremely friendly birds that may reward you with 150 eggs a year.

Orpington

One of the most popular breeds, the Orpington has an army of admirers, particularly in its Buff form. With its wonderful showy feather duster plumage, and lovely gentle nature, this is hardly surprising. Unfortunately I have  to say yet again that the search for the perfect show bird has damaged this breed's utility qualities, perhaps more so than any other. Whilst it will never match the achievements of its Victorian forebears, today's hens will probably still give you around 150-160 eggs a year, and a cock bird should make eight pounds, and possibly more. Several new colours are emerging, although not as yet accepted for show standards, and the likelihood is that this favourite will continue to grow in popularity.

Plymouth Rock

Another product of the American quest for excellence, the Plymouth Rock is a good bird for beginners as it settles well in most situations, and is friendly and docile. An all-rounder, it produces a reasonable quantity of eggs, and is a medium sized meat bird. The Buff, as with all buff coloured poultry, has its loyal devotees, and the Barred variety is particularly striking.

Rhode Island Red

These hardy birds were produced in America during a spell in the late 1800s when they were striving to produce the perfect utility bird.

The results were rather successful as the best strains of this striking chicken will knock out around 220 eggs a year in their prime, and the cock will still reach weights approaching nine pounds. This quest for egg laying qualities was achieved at the expense of broodiness, however, and you will probably have to use a foster mother or incubator to produce your own chicks.

Sussex

This breed reached its peak during the 1930s when it be- came the table bird of choice for the British market. The birds were renowned for their egg laying ability too, produc- ing over 200 eggs a year in their heyday. The arrival of hybrids and factory farming led to their decline as meat birds, and the search for a good show bird sadly lost a little of their egg laying skills, but a good strain

will still manage 170 to 180 a year. They are gentle, inquisi- tive creatures and will happily follow you around the garden as you are pulling up weeds or digging. Of course, they have ulterior motives because they are searching for tasty titbits, but you can easily convince yourself that they love you.

There are seven recognised colours for showing, but it can't be long before the Coronation, possibly the most beautiful of them all, is accepted.

Welsummer

The 1920s and '30s were a peak period for poultry development around the world, and the Welsummer was one of the results of Dutch endeavours in this direction. This perky, friendly little bird will provide you with a good supply of dark brown eggs,

provided that you obtain your stock from a good bloodline, and cock birds will produce a reasonable sized carcass. The good egg laying flighty side of their makeup means that they seldom go broody, and so you should plan to hatch young with a foster mother or incubator. The grass is always greener on the other side for a Welsummer, so you may need to clip a wing or cover their enclosure to keep them where you want them!

Wyandotte

Another product of the US search for perfection, this lovely breed comes in a strikingly beautiful range of amazing colours. Meat and egg production figures are very similar to the Sussex, and the colours available are certainly a major factor for many keepers, but we personally didn't like the rose comb. A silly thing to put us off, I know, and I'm sure that one day I will go back to them as I love their colours, particularly the Blue Laced variety. They are certainly an ideal bird for the breeder looking for the perfect bird for his garden – an attractive focal point, and lots of eggs. Their pleasant nature, hardiness and all-round ease of management make them an ideal beginner's bird.

Chapter Three

Housing

There are almost as many different types of houses and runs on the market as there are chicken keepers! The type that you should go for depends on the amount of space that you have available, and how much room you want to give to your chickens. This may sound a bit strange to you, but you have to remember that the main reason we started keeping chickens in the first place is an ethical one – we disagree with how most commercial chickens are raised.

We have used several different types of houses, and found that some of them really aren't suitable for the number or type of birds that the manufacturers state will fit into them. Their estimates are usually based on the roosting capacity of the housing, and don't always take account of the practicalities of other aspects such as run size, placement of feeders etc. If in doubt, halve the number of birds that they say are suitable.

When we bought our very first chickens we were sold a double-decker ark. It had a covered floor area approximately four feet square, with an upper deck that supplied roosting space and a nest box. A drop-down slatted ramp provided the birds with access between the two levels. An optional extra (which we didn't buy) was an extension to the run that doubled the ground floor area.

We were told that it was suitable for four large fowl or five bantams, and we tried both those combinations at different times. It wasn't really suitable for large fowl as they would more or less crash land each morning when the ramp was lowered, and they barely had headroom to roost, needing to lie horizontally across the perch. We used this ark purely as an overnight hotel for our chooks, and during the day they free ranged in the garden, and for this it was adequate. To keep them in it all the time, even with the extra run, you would have to reduce the number of birds drastically and keep moving the whole thing around the garden every few days to keep the soil fresh. Because of this arks usually have carrying handles to make moving them around easy for two people.

Many of the smaller houses are really only suitable for permanent use if they are moved regularly, and even a large house and run should ideally be re-sited annually if at all possible as the ground becomes stale.

Don't get me wrong, I'm not saying that arks or similar houses don't have a place in poultry keeping because they certainly do. We sold the double-decker to a friend of ours, together with three Sussex bantams, and it has proved to be ideal for this many birds.

Depending on size they are perfect for a breeding pair or trio (cock and two hens), or for a mother hen and her brood of chicks. Whether birds should be kept in them permanently is a matter of opinion – mine is personally that the very small arks aren't suitable.

Now that our poultry are kept on allotments we have a lot more space available, and we prefer to adapt garden sheds to our own specification. A 6´ x 4´ garden shed, with two perches fitted lengthwise, will comfortably hold 12 large fowl birds provided that there is a good sized outside run, but we prefer to give our birds even more space if at all possible. Remember that on a wet and miserable day the birds will probably stay inside, and should have sufficient room to be able to scratch around and feed, whilst still avoiding those above them in the pecking order.

Our main unit is now an 8′ x 6′ shed with a 15′ x 10′ run attached. In this we keep one large cockerel and six of his ladies, and they have plenty of room. There are perches both in the run and for roosting inside the shed, and an old section of shed is stood leaning at an angle against one side fence. This gives the birds some shelter from the wind and rain and allows them to stay outside in all weathers, not that getting wet seems to do them any harm or bother them. They are often out when it is pouring with rain and get soaked to the skin, but we haven't lost one yet because of it, so don't worry that you have to pamper or fuss over them too much.

A 6 x 4 shed can make an ideal chook house. Note the external nestboxes, with access via a liftable lid, which frees up space inside the shed, the straw-covered scratching area, and the netting over the run.

The sheltered area also ensures that a patch of ground is kept dry for them to use as a dust bath. Dust bathing is an essential activity for chickens – factory farmed poultry will pathetically try to dust bath in the sawdust in their cages. The dust helps them to keep free of parasites (more about these later) and there is no doubt that they enjoy doing it. Several times I have come across birds apparently lying dead in their dust baths, only for one beady eye to open and peer at me from the throes of ecstasy!

If you have a bonfire, spread the wood ash from it in their dust bath, as this is particularly effective in getting rid of

Providing dust bath facilities is absolutely essential for the good health of your poultry. Of course, given a choice, mum will always prefer to teach her chicks how to bathe in your favourite flower bed........
Even chicks two or three days old, reared without a mother, will attempt to dust bath in sawdust in their brooder, so it is clearly an instinctive urge.

mites on the birds. Do not use the ash from a coal fire, however, as it is possible that this can contribute towards the condition known as scaly leg.

The house should be dry and well ventilated, without causing direct draughts on the poultry. Your pop hole will provide an entry point for fresh air at ground level and provide some further vents by drilling holes at the apex so that there will be a good air flow. If you intend to shut your flock up at night (more on this later) then the pop hole needs to be fitted with a sliding door. One important point is that the door should slide vertically rather than horizontally. One badly designed house that we purchased early on had a horizontal door, and the grooves of the runner were constantly clogging up with mud and droppings deposited by the bird's feet as they

Site your feeders and drinkers in a position where they won't get fouled by the bird's droppings when they are roosting. The nest boxes are nicely secluded – and the one furthest from the door is the most popular with the girls. Since this picture was taken we have begun to use wood shavings as bedding in preference to straw, and the perches have been altered so that they fit into slots and can be removed

climbed in and out of the house. The slots were quite narrow too, and inaccessible, and the very devil to clean out.

The pop hole should not face the direction of your prevailing wind, as rain will get blown inside. Here, in East Anglia, we also avoid the north or east if at all possible, to avoid the really bitterly cold winds of winter.

If you are making use of a garden shed for your housing, it will probably be fitted with windows. These raise a few points that need to be discussed. If sited on an allotment you should bear in mind the security issue. If the shed, or at least the windows, are inside your run then there isn't a problem really. If, however, they are outside the run then they risk attacks from vandals. We haven't had a great deal of problems on our allotments, but broken shed windows have been one of them. You must cover your windows with a grill or netting to prevent them being broken. Remember that a broken window may allow your birds to escape, or worse, give a fox an easy way in.

Try not to position your shed in such a way that the windows face south, as the interior will become very hot and stuffy when the sun is shining strongly. If the windows face into the run it would be very beneficial to remove the glass and fit wire netting in its place, with shutters on the outside. These can then be opened during the daytime to allow plenty of fresh air and light, and closed again in the evening. During hot summer weather the shutters can be left open overnight. The point about not facing pop holes into the prevailing wind applies equally, in fact more so, to windows if you remove the glass, as the interior can very quickly be awash in heavy rain.

Your chicken housing can be as simple or as ornate as you like. Our own allotment field is rapidly becoming a shanty town of sheds and chicken houses cobbled together as more and more new people take over the plots and decide to keep a few chickens. It all adds to the charm of the place, and the odd home-made monstrosity doesn't really matter too much.

In your garden things are a bit different though, as you want your garden to look attractive. You either have to get housing that is aesthetically pleasing, or tuck it away at the bottom of the garden and screen it with bushes, hedging or fencing. You are almost certainly going to want to be able to observe your chickens as they go about their daily lives though, and so most people opt for a professionally built house and run for their garden. But remember that pretty isn't the important part – practicality and the welfare of your

Allotments have always had a shanty town appearance, with lots of sheds in various conditions, but the current boom in chicken-keeping has led to all manner of housing being erected, adding to the effect. Most of the runs on our allotments have been built using steel fencing panels as there is a plentiful local supply from building sites.

stock is the prime factor. The boom in garden poultry has led to a glut of houses on the market, made by people who can barely nail two pieces of wood together, and who have clearly never kept chickens or considered their welfare.

An attractive house is no use if you can't clean it out easily or dismantle parts of it to get at all the nooks and crannies if the dreaded red mite strike – and if they do then you don't want to have to poke your head into the house to disinfect it. Nest boxes should have easy access and feeders and drinkers need a spot where they won't be fouled by roosting birds – the amount of droppings produced by chickens whilst at roost is amazing, around half of their daily output. An easily-removable droppings board that fits under the roosting perches is certainly a boon to cleaning. Consider all these points carefully before buying that twee little house that looks so charming. Also consider providing a fully covered run. Not only does this provide defence against the disease avian influenza, but it will prevent the run turning into a swamp in heavy rain. This will be better for the birds, help to keep eggs clean, and prevent the centre point of your garden from   turning into a stinking eyesore.

A house that can be totally dismantled like this model is pretty much perfect when it comes to cleaning and disinfecting needs. If you get an attack of red mite – and you almost certainly will at some point – then you need to strike hard to clear them, and get into every nook and cranny.

When it comes to both birds and housing, don't buy the first thing that you see, but shop around. Listen to what the sellers tell you, and think about it. Sellers want to sell, and won't always tell you the full story or the truth.

Flashy websites are similarly angled at selling, although there are some very informative ones out there on the internet. Ask questions, and see how much time and advice your seller is prepared to give you, as this will give an indication of how much time he will have to help you later if you encounter problems. Remember that they will probably be busy and have lots of other people to talk to, and myriad jobs that need to be done, so don't expect to monopolise their time.

If you are thinking of keeping a couple of hens in the garden, just for a few eggs, then you could consider one of the new ultra-modern eglu's manufactured by the Omlet Company. This innovative idea provides a house with nesting and roost-

ing areas, all made of insulated polymer. The whole thing can be dismantled for cleaning, so you can thoroughly disinfect the whole thing. An attached run incorporates outward-turned base panels to prevent a fox from digging his way in, and you can move the whole thing around your garden every couple of days to give your chooks fresh ground to peck over.

Personally, I wouldn't want to house more than 3 birds in one, but if you are looking

Not many people could spare the space in their garden for the chicken house in the top picture, or the money to buy it. However, the smaller house below would look good in anybody's garden and create a home fit for a king for your chooks. I particularly like the fully covered run, with a roof constructed of onduline rather than felt, as this won't provide a sheltered home for the dreaded red mite. With the ever-present risk of avian influenza,

for an attractive talking point feature for your garden, this could be it.

Alternatively, you could use one as a broody coop/chick run and have hours of enjoyment watching the chicks and mum in your garden, knowing that they are safe. They are not cheap, but then again neither is a lot of the housing being retailed these days.

Whichever type of housing you go for, rule number one is that it must be fox proof. These crafty creatures will find their way round many defences, and if all else fails they will chew through a wooden door to get to a nice two-legged meal. If they get inside your henhouse they will kill everything inside it in a matter of minutes. They go into a frenzy and just kill anything that moves. Afterwards, if they are left undisturbed, they will remove the dead birds one at a time and take them away.

One chicken keeper on our allotments lost thirteen hens in one night, and they were all found dotted around the field buried in shallow scrapes for later retrieval. All the birds taken were defenceless hens that had gone broody and were sitting on eggs at ground level. The cockerels, which were roosting high up, were untouched. Broody hens go into a kind of trance, and will not leave their eggs no matter what happens.

I considered our runs to be pretty much bomb proof, but even then a wily fox found his way in one night. Our main house now sits on a concrete slab, and others have solid wooden floors. Where walls have been a bit weak I have nailed feather edge boarding over them to strengthen them. Generally it is the runs that are the danger area.

Our first one was built using six foot high two inch chicken wire on three inch square posts. The wire was taken right over the top, and all joins thoroughly stitched together using strong wire.

I then excavated all the soil from inside to a depth of three inches, and laid overlapping sheets of chainlink fencing all over the floor. These were stitched together, and to the sides, with strong wire. The soil was then replaced. This

It was a painstaking job, but well worth the effort. A heavy gauge wire was nailed to the top of the fence posts, and both the side netting and the chicken wire over the run were very carefully and securely stitched to it, creating a foxproof home for our Light Sussex girls.

may sound extreme, but a fox has never breached the defences of this run. I did, however, realise that the hens will stick their heads out through the holes to eat anything in reach (the grass is always greener.......) and a couple of allotment holders had their hens' heads bitten off by wily, stalking predators, so I added some two feet high wire with half inch holes all the way round at ground level. I now consider Colditz to be pretty safe from foxes – although a badger could chew its way straight through chicken wire, and rats, ferrets or mink could probably get through the two inch holes higher up.

If you get into chicken raising at the level we did you will soon find that you need extra runs to grow on your chicks

Chicken wire, or better still chainlink fencing, set six inches into the ground and out two feet from the base of your fence will stop a fox from digging his way into your runs.

and youngsters. We found that the quickest and easiest way of doing this was using the steel fencing panels that are used to surround building sites. These often get sold off cheaply at the end of a job, and hire companies sell any that have been slightly damaged. They are great for erecting a quick, solid structure. Once the walls are up you need to dig out a trench all the way round. It only needs to be about six inches deep and two feet wide. You then put up wire netting all the way round the base, taking it down into the trench, and across the bottom. You then fill in the trench and secure the netting to your fencing every foot or so using wire or cable ties.

When a fox tries to get into your run, it will always try to dig at the base of the fence, and six inches down will hit the wire netting and give up. Believe me, it works – we have had several attempted chicken dinner attacks, and they have all given up when they reached the wire. Our extra runs do not have the floor fully wired, and the only fox that ever got in dug completely under a shed and popped up in the run, because I had not thought to sink wire into the ground along the inside bottom edge of the shed. We were lucky as he only took one chicken from a shed full. Needless to say, that oversight was quickly rectified!

Nylon netting stretched across our runs and attached securely prevents unwelcome visitors. The one drawback is that when it gets very wet it sags badly, however tightly stretched, and you get a soaking from it when you go about your duties.

We finished them off by stretching nylon fish netting over the top. If you think that this is unnecessary with six foot high fencing, think again – we use the same fencing for our goats and foxes have gotten into their pens, which are not covered.

One measure that more and more poultry keepers are resorting to nowadays is electric fencing. Certainly a wire placed around the top of six foot high run fencing is generally enough to keep Mr Fox away.

If your chickens are in your garden, then obviously mains electricity is likely to be available. On an allotment you are likely to have to resort to a battery-powered system. In this case you have to ensure that the batteries are always fully charged, as foxes seem to be able to sense when the power is off. I personally can place my hand close to an electrified wire and can feel the energy field, and I have no doubt whatsoever that a fox's whiskers or nose are similarly sensitive.

It is widely believed that a second wire is needed just above ground level, but I would dispute this. Provided that you have buried wire netting below ground level at the base of your fences, and brought it out two feet then no further protection is needed. Ground level electric fencing is in any case extremely vulnerable to shorting out caused by long grass or weeds. Surrounding undergrowth needs to be constantly cut back or your wiring will be ineffectual. Don't forget that low-hanging tree branches can similarly short circuit your fencetop wiring.

Chicken runs, if unroofed, should be positioned ten feet away from any other tall object, whether you have used an electrified wire or not. Foxes will jump onto anything stacked, or a nearby shed roof or tree, and use it as a springboard to get over your fencing. I really cannot overstress the cunning of foxes, and you should give them great respect. Try to think like a fox and look at your housing through their eyes.

Also please don't assume that your pretty little manufactured chicken house will be fox proof too. Very few have floors in the run section, and it will only take a fox a matter of moments to dig under the sides.
If in doubt, tack some wire netting to the underside of your ark or run. It won't stop the hens from pecking around, but may well save their lives.

Just because you live in a town doesn't mean that you won't have foxes in your garden – in fact you are now more likely to have a visit from Old Reynard in a town than in the countryside. They seem to know that fox hunting has now been banned and have moved into towns in large numbers, where a lot of kind-hearted but misguided people feed them. The easy food makes them lazy hunters, and they look around for other easy meals – don't let it be your poultry!

Similarly, they are no longer purely nocturnal hunters, and I have seen them on our allotments at all hours of the day. They have very little fear of humans, and when they have a burrow full of five or six hungry cubs whining for food they can get desperate.

If you are letting your garden hens into the run in the morning, and closing them up in their house just before dark, you can probably get away with not covering the run, provided the side fences are high, and also not bother setting wire netting into the ground. Be aware, however, that the day you are delayed getting home from work, and arrive back just half an hour after sunset, may well prove to be the day that old foxy goes out hunting early, and your chooks are now greasing his chin. So many people that I know have lost chickens to foxes, I don't believe it is worth taking any chances.

It is my honest opinion that any chicken run should be covered to provide maximum protection.

Having discussed security for your birds, I have to mention vermin of a different kind – the two-legged variety. Poultry have a cash value and a food value. Anybody desperate for either is likely to be tempted by your birds. Low-level security is generally sufficient for your garden, but if you are setting up chicken housing on allotments then it needs to be very secure. Housing and runs need to be locked with strong doors, fittings and locks. Small, free-standing housing is not really viable unless locked inside a secure compound as birds and housing are likely to disappear.

If you keep game birds such as Old English Game or Indian Game, then your security needs to be doubly tight, even at home – perhaps indeed more so, as these breeds are targets for unscrupulous folk looking for suitable birds for cock-fighting. Although this practice has long been illegal, don't be naïve and imagine that it has disappeared, because it hasn't. Don't under any circumstances advertise spare cockerels for sale in local newspapers, as you are likely to attract unwanted visitors when you are not around.

Returning to general housing issues, you need to allow a minimum of twelve inches of roosting perch for each bird, and more if you have the space. They will generally sleep all huddled together, but there needs to be room for birds that are being bullied to find a spot to sleep. The perches are best made from 2″ x 2″ wood, and the square edges should be rounded off, or your birds will end up with sore feet. They should be no more than 12 inches from floor level, especially if you are keeping large fowl, as they can damage muscles or tendons jumping down onto a hard floor, or develop a painful condition known as bumblefoot.

Having said that, chickens like to roost as high as possible, and light breeds will fly up to the highest point that they can reach. One way of sorting out roosts to suit everybody is to arrange them in tiers, stepping up like a ladder. Even the heavy birds can hop up from the lowest to the top this way. For obvious reasons the perches should not be directly above one another. If you choose this method, you must, however, ensure that there is ample room on the top perch for all your flock, as they will all want to claim a spot on the highest point, and there will be terrible fights if they can't all get there. For this reason, if not installing the ladder system, all low-level perches should be at exactly the same height. High perches can possibly have a slight advantage in winter, as warm air rises, so a chicken roosting close to the roof will stay warmer.

The perches should fit into slots or recesses so that they can be removed for cleaning. Any crack or crevice is likely to become a home to red mite. More on these pests later, but they very quickly became the bane of our henkeeping lives!

You should provide secluded nest boxes for your hens so that they feel safe and secure to lay their eggs. Ideally, there should be one nest box for every three or four hens, although you can be absolutely sure that even if you have a dozen boxes they will all still try to lay their eggs in the same one – usually the one furthest from the door or in the darkest corner. Pieces of sacking or similar material hung across the opening can help, as the birds push their way past and then feel safe and cosy in the seclusion created.

You will find it more convenient if you can access your eggs from outside the house via a door or hatch. There really isn't a need for anything elaborate though – my chickens have gotten by very well in the past with cardboard boxes with a hole cut in the side! This isn't as mad as it sounds, because if you get an infestation of mite or fleas or other vermin you can just burn the boxes and put fresh ones in place.

The ideal nest box size is twelve inches square. A large fowl will fit this nicely, but there won't be enough room for two to crowd in, with the risk of broken eggs from clumsy great feet. You can use a smaller size for bantams, but think carefully about it in case you later decide to keep large fowl, and then have to change everything. Two bantams sitting side by size don't present the same danger of broken eggs as they are smaller, lighter birds – with smaller feet!

Space can be saved by siting nest boxes under perches, with a removable shelf above the boxes to catch the droppings.

If you are forced to position your nest boxes off the ground you should provide a handy perch for them to get to first, so that they can hop into the nest from there.

The litter within the house should be dust-free softwood shavings, about six inches deep. If you have droppings boards fitted, as described above, the litter should keep fresh for at least three months, and more likely six months. Your nose will tell you when it needs to be changed – the smell of ammonia or any trace of dampness or mustiness is the clue.

Don't disregard second hand housing, as it can often be obtained very cheaply. Ask why it is for sale – often it is because the owner has lost all their chickens to a fox. If this is the case, find out how they gained entry and decide whether you can remedy the danger. As long as the housing is sound (remember that wood rots, especially when in contact with the ground) and well designed, there is no reason why you shouldn't grab yourself a bargain.

Any secondhand housing should be thoroughly cleansed before use, as there may well be eggs of pests or diseases hiding in crevices, even if the house hasn't been used for a long time. Real creosote is no longer available for domestic use, but is sometimes available from agricultural suppliers. It is by far the best way to eradicate this danger, applied generously to both inside and outside surfaces, especially nooks and crannies. Allow the house to dry thoroughly, and fumes to clear, before letting your chickens anywhere near it.

If you can't obtain real creosote, then a strong solution

of Jeyes Fluid is the next best remedy, sprayed liberally, especially on joints.

If at all possible your feeders and drinkers should be inside the house, and definitely under cover. Avian Influenza keeps rearing its ugly head in this country, and the problem is not going to go away. It seems that the disease is spread largely through droppings from wild birds, and so it is essential that you keep them away from your chicken's food and drink. You should also bear in mind that if there is an outbreak near you, and you are in a protection or surveillance zone, then you will be forced to keep your birds under cover and away from contact with wild birds. If you can build your run with a good solid roof right from the start then so much the better, but a well secured tarpaulin is acceptable to DEFRA, the government body overseeing animal health. We have rolls of fruit cage netting ready to wrap round our runs to keep the wild birds out if it becomes necessary. We actually experienced being in a surveillance zone when there was an AI outbreak nearby, but we didn't need to use the netting. Luckily it occurred at a time of year when we had no flocks of youngsters, just our basic breeding stock, and so we were able to cope by confining them indoors in their sheds with no ill effects or hardship for the birds.

We were also at the centre of the first ever Bluetongue outbreak at the time, and also foot and mouth had escaped from the government research centre at Pirbright, and as we have goats as well as poultry it was an extremely worrying time for us. Our goats had actually been due to be mated at the farm where the BT outbreak started.

Incidentally, having mentioned DEFRA, you should be aware that if you keep more than fifty birds you will have to register for the UK Poultry Register. There has been much talk in some circles that you should keep your numbers below the registration level, but we feel that this is unfounded. DEFRA are somewhat feared because of their "kill everything" attitude if there is a disease outbreak close by your premises, but not being registered would not protect you from their attentions in any case. Fearful neighbours would be sure to inform the authorities if they felt that their own health was threatened. It seems likely that the need to be registered will eventually be extended to cover all poultry keepers anyway, in which case the argument would be pointless. Yes, you could face the possibility of a health check inspection from the men in white suits if you are registered, but if you are keeping your birds in good conditions (the aim of this book is, after all, ethical food) then you have nothing to worry about from such a visit.

We have digressed a little, so back to the subject of feeders and drinkers. Place drinkers away from the perches, so that the birds don't foul their own water with droppings, and try to get them off the floor a bit. We stand ours on plastic boxes about six inches high.

We suspend the feeders from the roof, so that the rim of the feeding edge is level with or just below the chicken's throat. This does help to keep the feed away from the attentions of vermin. You will never keep mice away, particularly on allotments, and so anything that deters them helps. Mice can jump quite spectacularly though, and we have even hung the feeders in such a way that the birds have to eat from their perches in order to keep the mice away from their feed. You have to be careful that all the birds can get to the feeder though, or one or two bully birds will hog the feeding positions and keep others away. If in doubt, hang more than one feeder to ensure that birds lower down the pecking order get their share.

When we moved our poultry to the allotments, we were

given access in the autumn to large quantities of fallen leaves. The council delivers them to the plots for us to turn into leaf mould, a great soil improver, and we built a large cage to store them in and let them rot down for a year or two. We found them to be an excellent floor covering for the chicken runs, which can get very muddy and boggy in wet weather.

A six inch layer of leaves solves the problem nicely, and a handful of corn thrown into the leaves occasionally will keep the chickens amused for hours as they scratch around looking for it. They will constantly turn the litter over in their search for tender titbits such as the worms and creepy crawlies that will take up residence, and this will help to keep it all fresh. The corn probably doesn't help the mouse problem at all, but we feel that it is worth the risk as the birds are happy – and as long as you don't overdo the amount of corn the birds will probably find it all before the mice get a look-in anyway. Incidentally, corn is very fattening, so you really shouldn't give more than a small handful every once in a while.

A fixed run is always likely to have problems with sour soil after a while, unless it is very large, and even then the area around the house will become a problem unless you take steps to avert the damage. The leaf litter certainly works for us, and when the supply doesn't arrive, as happens some years, we use straw in its place. A good deep layer of straw seems to work just as well, and indeed was the litter of choice in the farm poultry scratch yard of years gone by. Often the old methods are the best, although I have to admit that some of the husbandry methods employed were cruel and almost barbaric, such as caponising. Caponising involved the surgical removal of the cockerel's testes. Normal cockerel behaviour such as fighting and courting would then cease, and the castrated bird would grow considerably fatter. Thank-

Our chickens love it when we fill their runs with autumn leaves, and will spend all day scratching around looking for tasty titbits. The leaf mould helps to prevent the run turning into a quagmire in heavy rain, making it much more pleasant for your birds.....and you.

fully the practice of caponisation is now illegal in the United Kingdom, but strangely it is not illegal to sell capons, and they can be imported from abroad to be sold here, a curious anomaly in the law. Generally speaking though, the farmers of yesteryear knew a thing or two, and old poultry books often contain gems of knowledge that have been forgotten today.

Each autumn we dig out the runs as the ground level rises steadily through the year. The mixture of leaf mould, uneaten vegetables, weeds and chicken droppings produces wonderful compost that we spread over our vegetable beds and dig in.

One last point on outside runs – if, despite all your careful planning, an area of your run becomes a waterlogged bog, all is not lost. It is very easy to construct a simple soakaway that will deal with the problem. When conditions are dry, simply dig a hole about two feet square and three feet deep at the lowest point of the affected area.

Chickens with feathered feet, such as Brahmas and Cochins, require special care to keep them in good condition. This thoughtful owner has filled the run with a deep layer of bark chips to prevent it turning into a mudbath. Photo: Jakki Keeble

Fill it about a foot deep with rubble and large stones, and pour fine gravel over this – the gravel will trickle down between the rubble and fill the gaps. Add another foot or so of rubble and again top up with gravel, then more rubble and fill with soil, stamping down firmly until level with the surrounding surface - This should take care of all but the most severe downpours.

Chapter Four

Feeding

A gain because of vermin, you should keep all your stored feedstuff in lidded bins, preferably metal ones. If you are unlucky enough to get a visit from rats, they are quite capable of chewing through plastic dustbins, and mice will chew through plastic or paper feed sacks.

When you buy your young stock, find out what the breeder has been feeding them with, so that you can continue with the same. The choice is pellets or mash. Pellets, as the name implies, are pelleted feed that includes all the trace minerals and elements that your birds will need to keep them healthy. Mash is similarly a balanced feed, but comes in a minced up form that can be served either dry or moistened with water. If you moisten it you won't be able to use flow feeders though, as it jams them up.

There are fans of both types of feed, with very convincing arguments for their preference, but we don't really feel that there is anything to choose between them, apart from a suspicion that if you use mash there may be a little more waste as choosy chickens may pick out their favourite snacks and leave the rest. Some say that mash takes the birds longer to eat and so keeps them occupied longer, but if you are giving plenty of other interesting food we feel that there is no need to worry. We feed pellets as we personally find them more convenient.

If your new purchases are quite young, they will probably still be fed with what are called growers pellets or mash. These contain a higher proportion of protein, to help the birds put on good growth. From about 18 weeks onward they should be switched to layers pellets or mash, which have a different mix, aimed more at promoting egg production. If your birds are still on growers, then they need to be gradually weaned onto layers by adding an increasing amount of layers over a period of about a week. This gives their digestion time to adjust. The same applies if you want to change them from pellets to mash or vice versa – if you just suddenly present them with something different they might not even recognise it as food. Don't start giving layers pellets too early as it can actually slow down the start of egg laying.

All these feeds are available in organic versions, which can sometimes cost twice as much as non-organic types. The choice is yours.

Many of the layers feeds will contain some form of colorant, designed to give your egg yolk a nice yellow colour, but of course it is totally artificial. This, incidentally, is how supermarket egg yolks get their colour. If you feed your hens the way that we do, you will see a huge difference in this colour, and more importantly in their flavour.

Our birds get oodles of green stuff – just about every weed cleared from our allotments gets tossed into their pen, and they love them. We aren't particularly fussy about knocking soil off the roots either, and this gives them the chance of finding a nice tasty worm or grub, so there is generally a rugby scrum when we have been weeding. They will particularly appreciate a large turf dug up and dumped whole in their run. We also hang cabbage, sprouts and cauliflower stems, complete with outer leaves, in their run. The outcome is the most glorious deep orange egg yolks that taste simply superb.

The poultry love it when we are digging our vegetable patches, as any bugs, beetles grubs etc that we find are usually thrown into their runs and eaten with gusto. They

You shouldn't let your chickens out in open areas like this unless you are able to keep an eye on them, and are absolutely certain that you can get them back into their runs easily. Our birds will do anything for some corn, so it is easy to lead them back home like the Pied Piper.

rarely eat caterpillars though, and you should never give them hairy caterpillars as the hairs often contain an irritant.

We also like to let them out of their runs when we are working, and they welcome the chance to get at some of the pests in our soil. If you are able to free range your birds, even in just a small area of your garden, they will obtain a huge amount of nutrition, trace elements and vitamins from the many small creatures, seeds and green stuff that they will forage. Your feed bill will also be slightly reduced as they will eat fewer pellets or mash. They will always prefer to find natural foods in preference to concentrated feed, but you mustn't think that because you free range them that they don't need pellets or mash. These feeds should always be provided on an ad lib basis.

All our chickens are given lots of vegetables from our allotments. Here our Sussex growers are tucking into a lettuce that had gone to seed. Small quantities that are eaten quickly can be thrown in the run, but larger amounts should be hung singly or placed in baskets to prevent

If you have a compost heap in your garden your chickens will be drawn to it like bees to a honey pot, because of the myriad wildlife living in it. They will scratch and dig in the heap all day, given the opportunity.

Household scraps are also something that can be fed to your stock to help reduce feed costs. All our potato peelings are saved in a saucepan, together with clippings from root vegetables such as carrots, swedes and parsnips, plus the outer discarded leaves of cabbages, cauliflowers etc, and all boiled up together.

The chickens love them. Left-over boiled, roasted or baked potatoes are also devoured greedily, but raw potatoes should never be given. Root vegetables can also be grated and fed raw. The cores of sweetcorn cobs, after the grains have been trimmed off, are a great favourite. Thinking about it, our chickens enjoy all the same vegetables that we do!

Do not, however, feed anything strongly flavoured to your egg layers – the taste can be passed on through their eggs.

As already mentioned, our poultry are fed huge amounts of weeds, as we have a quarter of an acre of allotments, and there are also many weed-choked abandoned corners in the surrounding plots. We are careful not to include any Bella Donna (Deadly Nightshade) or Groundsel because they are known to be harmful, and thistles or stinging nettles because

Your birds will love you if you dig a turf and throw it in their run. They will be as interested in digging in the soil for grubs as they are in eating the grass. It will keep them amused and active, which is just as important as the nutrition they obtain. Boredom can lead to problems like feather pecking, which is very difficult to stop once it has started.

the chickens won't eat them, but just about everything else goes into our two-legged composting system. Our goats, however, do love nettles and thistles though, so nothing gets wasted!

When feeding greenstuff such as cabbage leaves it is better to place it in a wire basket fixed to the wall so that the birds can pick away at it, rather than throw it on the floor, where it can quickly become soiled with droppings.

There is always something that you can do to put variety and little extras into their diet. For instance, we have scattered grass seed into seed trays full of soil, and then placed the whole tray into the chicken runs when the grass has grown to about an inch tall. Maize can be soaked in water and then left for a few days to germinate and sprout before being feed to your stock. The possibilities are endless.

One very important thing to remember is to start feeding any new food to your chickens in moderation. If their digestion is not used to it, anything new can cause terrible scouring (diarrhoea) for the birds, and it can very easily prove fatal. Start them off on small quantities and then gradually increase the amount over a few days.

The other item that you must ensure that your poultry have an adequate supply of is grit – small sharp stones. Strange as it sounds, the birds swallow grit whole. It is absolutely crucial to their digestion, as they use it in their gizzard to grind up their food, which is swallowed whole as they have no teeth. The grit eventually wears down to tiny pieces and passes through the bird's system. If they have good access to an outside run where they can dig and scratch they will find their own, but in a permanent run they can pretty much clear the area of suitable grit over time, so more should be supplied.

After swallowing food enters the crop, a kind of holding area where it is moistened and softened. It then travels to the stomach, which consists of two halves. The first part, the proventriculus, is where acidic juices begin breaking the food down. It then passes to the gizzard, where strong muscular walls contract and work with the grit to grind the food up. Tough food like maize or other hard seeds will pass backwards and forwards several times between the two halves until broken down enough to pass on into the digestive system.

Without a good steady supply of grit your stock will not get the full nourishment that they need from their food, as it will not be sufficiently broken down to release all its goodness.

You should also give them oyster shell grit, and this will be doubly useful as it contains calcium which will be absorbed by their bodies and be used in the production of their eggshells, preventing problems with soft-shelled eggs. Don't forget that even young chicks need grit once they are around seven days old, albeit smaller stones. They might not take it from a separate dish, so mix it in with their crumbs.

Another way is to recycle the eggshells – we keep all the shells of eggs that we use, and then pop them under the grill when we have something cooking in the oven below. This bakes them nice and brittle, and we then crush them and feed them back to the birds. This serves two purposes – assisting with their digestion and helping to prevent soft shells. Waste not want not is our motto.

Oyster shell grit should be provided in hoppers to keep it dry, or in dishes inside their house. Granite and flint grit can be sprinkled around their run.

Wheat, corn and other extras should be given very sparingly

as they are extremely fattening. Corn-fed birds are sold quite expensively in the shops, and considered to be a delicacy. That may be so, but we feel that it is best left to the experts as you can easily get the amount wrong. Chickens are not like pet dogs that look fat if you feed them too much. Outwardly they show very little, but when you slaughter them you will find that their chest cavity is full of fat, and the heart totally encased in it. There will also be bright yellow fat under the skin around the neck. A build up of fat will seriously affect the hen's egg production, may result in her getting egg-bound and dying, and will seriously reduce a cockbird's fertility and effectiveness. As with humans, it can also cause heart attacks.

It is also better to give mixed corn than plain wheat.

Water is essential, and should be available at all times. Whilst open containers such as bowls can be used, they will very quickly be contaminated by the bird's droppings. It is much better to use plastic or metal fountains that can hold a good volume and keep it clean.

Plastic founts are cheaper, but over a period of time can become brittle and shatter if knocked or dropped. They also become coated with algae on the inside when the sunlight penetrates the opaque plastic. This is unsightly, but harmless. Metal fountains last for many years, but do eventually rust. Never use water from ponds, water butts or any other standing source as it may introduce microscopic parasites to your birds' guts. Fresh, clean tap water is the only type to use, but there is no need to change it daily as I have seen claimed elsewhere. It is important to keep an eye on the water level though, and completely refill the container when it gets low. Your chickens should never be without water, and like us they drink more in hot weather.

If the water fountain is positioned inside their house, the warmth of the birds' bodies may be enough to prevent the water freezing in mildly frosty weather, but in a severe cold snap the drinkers may freeze up solid. Do not attempt to crack open plastic drinkers using force, as they become brittle in the cold and may shatter. Standing them in a washing up bowl full of hot water is the simplest means of sorting out the problem. Get on with any other jobs that need doing and leave them to soak for a few minutes. Refill the drinker with warm water. If the daytime temperature stays below freezing you may need to do this two or three times during the day to ensure that water is always available.

Your birds will appreciate some wet mash in cold weather, mixed with warm water and any of the household scraps that I have previously mentioned.

Chapter Five

Breeding

The breeding season in the UK generally starts around late November when the birds have recovered from their annual moult, and continues until July time when they begin to moult again. This does, however, vary according to breed and climate, so should only be taken as a guideline.

Before starting your breeding operations in November you should give some thought to how you are going to raise your chicks. Serious show breeders who start early do so because they want to have birds mature enough to show the following year, and will probably have indoor runs in which to grow on their youngsters. If you hatch your young in November or December, how are you going to protect them when the cold and snow hits in January or February?

Traditional Easter cards often have pictures of young chicks on them, and to our minds this is the best time of year to start hatching if you want to raise several broods in the season. If one or two hatches are all that you intend to rear, then you can start even later in the year, although you should bear in mind that if your new youngsters haven't started laying by the end of August they probably won't do so until the following spring. Early in the season a cockerel's fertility is not high, so the later you can leave it, the better your results are likely to be.

One factor that seriously affects cock fertility and hen egg-laying is light. We don't like the cold, dark winter months, so why should our birds be any different? As soon as the days start to lengthen (and thus the time available for feeding/ foraging becomes longer) so the hens up their egg production and the cock's sperm production increases.

The way to get your breeding season started early is to provide artificial light; effectively to con the chickens into thinking the seasons are starting to change. It is easy enough to rig a light up to a time switch, but don't set it up to come on in the evening – if it switches off suddenly it may well catch the birds unprepared and they won't have gone to roost properly and will be caught on the floor in the dark. It is far better to have the light come on before dawn in the morning, and stay on until natural daylight appears. The optimum amount of light for perfect breeding conditions is around 14 hours a day.

I have already said that it is better to breed from second-year hens than from young pullets, and the same applies to your cockerel. Mature hens will not accept the attentions of an amorous young rooster, and will resist his advances. He will become frustrated and his attempts to mate will become more and more desperate, and fights will ensue.
A young rooster's fertility is also often poor, and so we have never used cockerels less than a year old for mating. The absolute ideal breeding combination is a one year old cock with a two year old hen.

We generally only use the cock bird for one season. By the time he is two years old he will have grown large sharp spurs on his heels, which can do considerable damage. These were the weapons central to the illegal 'sport' of cock-fighting. They were usually sharpened to do maximum damage to the opponent, or even fitted with razor-sharp metal spurs.

A mature cock's spurs can do considerable damage to the backs of the poor hens, and his favourite wives will end up with completely bald backs. If the cock bird is left with the hens this damage will rapidly deteriorate to a torn and bloody mess. It is possible to fit the hens with 'poultry saddles' -

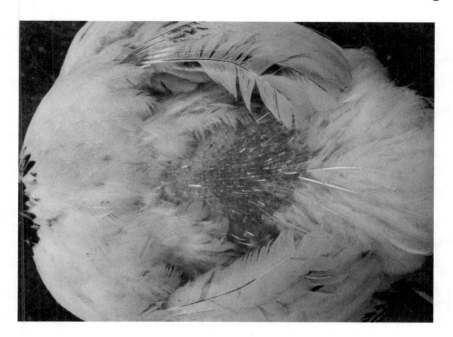

The cock bird's spurs can seriously injure the hens' backs during the mating season. If at all possible, it is better to house the cock birds separately, and only introduce them to the hens when you actually require fertile eggs. Allow ten days after putting the birds together

cloth or leather back protection that ties under the wings, or some keepers file down the spurs on the cockerels to blunt them. We prefer to use our cockerels for one season only, then house them in the freezer, and pick the best male offspring to continue as the next season's sire.

As soon as he is introduced to his girl, or girls, he will begin courting them by dropping a wing and dancing and display-ing around them.

This will quickly lead to mating – or to fighting if the female has a headache and is unwilling. Some of the more direct cockerels will miss out the courtship stage, grab the hen by the neck and jump aboard. A cockerel will mate irrespective of the weather conditions, and he is just as likely to trample his lady into the mud – chickens have no sense of etiquette! A favourite courtship technique is to creep up behind the hen when she is eating and pounce on her.

You should never ever keep a few hens with several cockerels. The poor girls have to run the gauntlet of the males to get to their roost at dusk, which is the favourite mating time for roosters, and it invariably leads to mass gang rapes that can leave the poor girls in a terrible state.

One cockerel can comfortably handle eight large breed females and still maintain his fertility. If you have a large flock then you should run more cocks with them, but they should have plenty of space to be able to escape one another or they may well fight to the death.

Hatching

Collect your hatching eggs daily and lightly mark the date laid in pencil on each one. If you keep several breeds or colours then you should also identify the egg with an "LS" for light Sussex or "SD" for Silver Dorking, for example, so that you can distinguish them later. This is particularly important if you are selling hatching eggs as your buyer will NOT be happy to hatch Light Sussex large fowl when he was expecting Silver Laced Wyandotte bantams!

When the time comes to incubate you will want to incubate the freshest eggs, hence the date mark. Eggs can be seven days old when you begin to incubate, and we have even had good hatch rates from ten day old eggs, but this is pushing it to the limits. There is a lot of waffle written about how you should store your eggs prior to incubating – that they need to be stored correctly at an evenly cool temperature, turned twice daily, stood a certain way etc etc etc ad nauseum. This is a simple book aimed at simply raising chickens, and I can tell you that we have never bothered with any of this hocus-pocus. Our eggs are stored in standard egg boxes and stood on the kitchen worktop until we are ready to hatch them. Our kitchen is not centrally heated, and the temperature varies according to the time of day and what cooking operations are going on. As there is often water running, and kettles and saucepans boiling, the humidity is probably fairly high. We have had excellent hatch rates, often 100%, so we feel that eggs are much tougher than people realise. In the wild a bird will not start incubating the eggs until it has laid a full clutch, and those eggs will be subject to the vagaries of temperature caused by the weather conditions.

It may be purely coincidental, but we have noticed that we get a fairly high percentage of hens from eggs stored this way. When we stored them in a cold outhouse we got quite a lot of boys from the hatch – and once, when we were forced by circumstances to hatch eggs that had been in the fridge a few days, we got 100% cockerels!!

If you really want to follow the standard procedure then store them pointed end downwards in egg boxes tipped at a 45° degree angle in a room at a constant 55°F (12°C) and turn the box round twice daily.

You should never keep badly soiled eggs for hatching, but slightly mucky or muddy ones are fine. Do not attempt to clean them before storage as this is best done at the start of incubation. Egg shells are covered with a fine bloom that helps to keep them fresh and protect them from infection. If you wash or wipe them this can be damaged and the egg can already be infected and starting to rot when you begin incubating. A bad egg placed in an incubator will often explode and spray the other eggs with a stinking mess that is full of germs. We had this happen once with an incubator full of expensive posted hatching eggs, and had only 3 eggs hatch from a batch of 24 eggs.

When selecting your final eggs for incubating, you should discard any eggs that are not perfectly oval. Some will be irregularly shaped, wrinkled, obviously thin-shelled or porous, and these should not be hatched. You are looking for the perfect egg with a nice healthy sheen to it. If this process leaves you with more eggs than you want to hatch you should then use those that were laid most recently, but do not use eggs laid that day – they need to have stood for 24 hours before being incubated. If you are using hatching eggs that have been posted to you, they also should all be stood until the day after receipt before incubating, to allow the contents to settle.

Just before you pop them under your hen or in the incubator you should clean the eggs using a proprietary incubation disinfectant. This is sold to sterilise incubators, but a diluted solution is ideal for cleaning eggs. One very important point is that the liquid should be at a very slightly higher temperature than the egg. The makeup of eggshells is such that if you wipe it with cold water the water will be sucked into the shell, taking any bacteria with it and infecting the egg. This does not happen with warm water. Slightly moisten a soft cloth and very gently wipe the surface of the egg, wiping off any dirty marks in the process. This should leave the whole surface of the egg sterile.

Now that you have your fertile eggs you have more decisions to make. There are two ways of hatching eggs, the natural way or in an incubator. The natural way can be the birds hatching their own eggs, or placing the eggs under another 'adoptive' hen that has gone broody. I can already hear you asking, "What's broody?"

When the weather gets warmer, and one day you go to collect your morning breakfast egg only to find a hen firmly ensconced in the nest box, refusing to move, screeching and squawking and pecking at your hands – that's broody! She has decided that she likes the eggs that you were going to have for breakfast and she will defend them against all comers. If you are ready to start breeding and want her to stay broody you should leave her with an egg or two, and remove any other eggs. The ones that you leave her with should be clearly marked in some way with a pencil so that you can distinguish them from eggs laid the next day, so that fresh ones can be removed on a daily basis. She needs to have sat for several days, and be quite determined about it, before you take her to the next stage. In the meantime you can be collecting up eggs from the birds that you wish to breed from.

Your chosen broody should be fit, healthy and nicely plump as sitting eggs is a long and arduous job, during which time she will eat very little, so she needs to be 100% fit for the job. Her comb should be nicely dark, and never under any circumstances use a broody affected by scaly leg mite.

Remember also that the timing has to be right for all factors to come together and work correctly. We have found it incredibly frustrating sometimes when all our bantam hens suddenly turn broody, when it is bantam eggs that we want to incubate this time round – and of course they don't lay when they are broody. Either that or we have broody bantams, and the large fowl that we wanted to breed from suddenly stop laying.....then they will come back into lay, but by then the bantams have given up sitting! That is when you give up and reach for the incubator. One thing that we have really noticed over the last few years is that very few of our large fowl seem to go broody, even the Sussex, which are reputedly one of the best sitters. Whilst the urge

This Crele Pekin has a good reason to camouflage himself in the undergrowth. His owner superglued the poor boys comb back on after it was severely damaged in a fox attack. Amazingly the emergency repairs did the trick and the lad was no worse for his misadventure – apart from a somewhat battered looking comb.
Photo: Paul Bates

to sit has been virtually bred out of many light breeds like Menorcas and Leghorns, it is a bit worrying that the amount of selective breeding practised now seems to be having an effect on the broodiness of utility strains. Incidentally, pullets rarely go broody in their first year, so don't expect too much of them.

Once your broody is sitting firmly, and you have collected enough hatching eggs in readiness, it is now time to move her to her permanent nesting site. You should never let a hen incubate eggs in the communal nest boxes; there is just too much going on there, with too many risks to the developing eggs. The chances are that she will be sitting in the flock's favourite laying box, and there will be constant squabbles

Although we set up our nests in the sleeping compartment of the rabbit hutch, I didn't say that they always stay there! This Coronation Sussex mum-to-be clearly wanted to be able to keep watch from the open side, and so shifted nest and eggs over to where she wanted them.

with other birds trying to get in to deposit their eggs. Whilst most sitting hens are quite amenable to others joining them – three birds crammed into a nest box at once is nothing unusual – it can result in addled or broken eggs. Similarly, the cockerel can take exception to her reluctance to come out for his regular mating and he can start a scuffle. All of this is detrimental to the peace and quiet that is needed for a high hatch rate.

There are various broody boxes and cages available, or you could make your own, but we have found the simplest and most effective thing to use is a rabbit hutch! We only use bantams as broodies, and so a smallish rabbit or guinea pig hutch is plenty big enough. If you are allowing a large fowl to hatch her own eggs, then you should obviously opt for

A brooding hen goes into a kind of trance as she sits quietly for hour after hour nursing her eggs. She will wake up quickly if danger threatens though, and peck quite savagely at your hands when you try to check up on the progress beneath her.

something more appropriate to give her sufficient room.

We set the sleeping compartment up as the nest, and the run is used as a feeding, watering and exercise area. The old way to create a nest was to cut a square of turf to fit the box, turn it upside down, put it in place and cut a hollow into it to form a cup to hold the eggs. This method helps to keep the humidity level quite high. Humidity is the amount of moisture suspended in the air, and the level is important when it comes to hatching time. We have tried incubating this way in the rabbit hutches, but we found that in hot, dry weather the turf dries out quickly, and you need to mist the nest lightly with tepid water to maintain the humidity level. As we do this anyway, we decided that the turf was pointless. The turf method was originally used in broody boxes that have no floor and stand directly on the ground,

so that the dampne...
used in this way it is ...
humidity.

If you decide to use the bro...
then of course you have to ...
predators and vermin by placing ...
preferably with a wire floor.

I'm not a big fan of the manufacture...
have no run. They are a basic box, and ...
no opportunity to leave the nest to eat, dr...
when it suits her. I prefer the natural way; a n...
to an exercise space, thus the rabbit hutches are ...
way that I work.

We place a layer of coarse wood shavings in the nestin...
in the rabbit hutches, and cover it with a thin layer of l...
hay.

If you use too much then the young chicks can get their feet tangled up in it and are unable to get back under mothers warm body, and so can die. Don't provide too deep a layer of shavings, or eggs will get buried and lost in it.

Your hen will literally be a sitting target for lice and more importantly mites whilst she is sitting in a dark nest box. It is good idea to give both her and the nest a good dusting with louse powder and also red mite powder. During one particularly hot summer we very nearly lost three sitting bantams that were overwhelmed by red mite overnight. In the evening when we inspected them they were fine, but the next morning they were almost at deaths door. If you have any suspicions, inspect the nest with a torch in the dead of night – if the poor girl is covered with tiny black specks you need to act fast!

he nesting
eggs from
and place
move her

reaking
. Walk
d eggs
sitting
ettled
from
h.

her
ad
eir

ss can permeate the nesting material, and
a very effective method of maintaining

ody box on the ground method,
protect the sitting hen from
the box inside a secure run,

d broody boxes that
the sitting bird has
nk and defecate
st with access
ideal for the

area
ght

out. They will
out once a day for a quick
to void their waste. This is generally in
form of one huge dropping that is easy to remove.

We choose to remove our broodies once a day to make sure that they are eating and voiding. If you do this, you should exercise great care when lifting them out of the nestbox. When we first started hatching I picked a hen up and lifted her out. As I did so I heard <plop> <plop>. Looking down I found two broken eggs that she had tucked firmly under her wings. It was heartbreaking as both eggs were close to hatching and contained healthy chicks. I never made the same mistake again! Lift your hen off the nest with a hand under her body, having first made sure that there are no eggs hidden there.

You will probably find that the hen will pull out quite a few of her breast feathers and line the nest with them. This serves two purposes; the soft lining helps to cushion the eggs and keep them insulated, and her bare breast passes more heat to the eggs.

Bantam eggs will generally hatch out after about 19 days, and large fowl after 21 days. This can vary slightly, according to temperature and humidity changes, but it is a good guide. Some eggs will hatch out a day or two after the rest if the hen is still sitting on them. Often the hen will leave the nest as soon as she has hatched off enough chicks to keep her happy, abandoning the remaining eggs. We have successfully hatched these by quickly popping them in the incubator or under another hen that is sitting.

Some breeders do not agree with this, and I have witnessed some big arguments on the subject. Their theory is that if the chick doesn't hatch out on time it is because it hasn't developed properly or has a defect of some kind, and that because of this they shouldn't be raised and used for breeding. I suspect that there is some truth in this, as the hens themselves operate a system of natural selection – the strongest hatch and survive and are led away, the others are left behind. If this were a book about raising and exhibiting poultry at shows, and establishing your own blood lines, then I would be inclined to agree. It is, however, a book aimed at people who want to raise their own meat and eggs in an ethical way, and so I will tell you that we do everything to ensure a good hatch, sometimes waiting two days for late hatchers, and will assist a chick that is having trouble getting out of the shell.

Humidity is a critical factor, and if a chick is a little slow hatching the inner egg membrane will dry out quite quickly, sticking to the chick and very effectively imprisoning it in the egg. However strong the chick is, it will not be able to turn within the shell to chip its way all round and pop the end off the egg. I'm not the sort of person that can watch something die needlessly, and so I intervene at this stage and give a little help by picking away some of the shell. You should never completely remove the chick from the shell, however, as it will probably bleed to death shortly afterwards. The chick is connected to the egg membrane by an umbilical chord from its rear end, and there seems to be something that takes place in the final struggles of getting out of the shell that closes down this connection and stops the blood flow.

I should stress that under no circumstances do we sell or breed from any of these late hatchers. They are fattened for the table.

As already mentioned, the hen will often leave the nest once she considers that enough chicks have hatched, and so you can end up with a small brood – possibly too small to raise efficiently. We have our own solution to this problem. We wait until we have two or three hens sitting solidly, and save up enough eggs to pop under them when we are ready, but also enough to fill our incubator. The one we use holds 20 eggs, and we start them off incubating on the same day that we put the hatching eggs under the hens.

All the chicks will generally hatch out within a 24 hour spell. Nature will take its course with those eggs under the broodies, and what will be will be, but at home in the incubator we generally get close to a 100% hatch as long as the eggs are fertile. The chicks at home are moved into a brooder for 24 hours or so until they are strong, and eating and drinking well. Just before dusk they are transferred to a box and taken to the nesting hens, who are now sitting on chicks. It is an easy matter to share the chicks out amongst them, holding them inside your cupped hand and pushing them underneath their new mum. The sitting birds don't bat an eyelid, except perhaps to peck at you to protect their chicks, and in the morning don't seem to notice that they have more babies – chickens clearly can't count! It is easy to share out twenty chicks between two or three sitting hens with no problems. This way you are assured of good-sized broods, and don't have the inconvenience of keeping them warm and looked after, as their foster mother does all this for you.

After a few days, when the chicks are strong and running around freely, the hen and chicks are transferred to a grower run. These are houses with an attached run, where the chicks can run around and get fit and healthy, but quickly get under mum if they are cold or danger threatens. It is important that there is a covered area in the run, so that they can shelter from both sun and rain.

Food and drink should be provided either in the house or under the covered section, to prevent fouling by wild birds. For the first couple of weeks only chick crumbs should be offered, and both mother and chicks will eat them. After two weeks, if the chicks are large fowl, we generally start providing grower pellets and a little corn for the hen, and the chicks will also start to help themselves to these. Over the next few weeks you can wean the chicks onto grower pellets and stop offering chick crumb by the time that they are six weeks old. Bantam chicks, being smaller, may choke on pellets or corn, and so we don't offer them until the young are four weeks old. It is important to keep feeding the chick crumbs for six weeks (assuming that they have a coccidiostat additive) in order for the young to be protected from coccidiosis, which is discussed elsewhere.

Incubating eggs is fairly straightforward with the modern designs that are available today, and we have had good results with even the most basic of machines. The modern

We started off with a simple incubator like this one, but without the autoturn cradle. A machine like this is called 'semi-automatic' because it is designed so that you manually turn the whole incubator several times a day, rather than having to turn all the eggs individually by hand.

machines generally have electronic thermostats rather than the old wafer type contact switches. These were inaccurate because they generally didn't switch off until a couple of degrees or so above the designated temperature, and the same with switching on. This could sometimes mean that the temperature swung wildly through a five or six degree range, badly affecting hatch rates. The contacts in the wafer thermostats would also sometimes fuse together, cooking your hatching eggs.

We started off with a machine borrowed from a friend. It didn't have a turning cradle or auto-turn mechanism, and the whole apparatus had to be turned by hand three times a day. This may sound cumbersome, but in some of the really basic machines you have to turn each individual egg by hand, so it was quite a clever piece of equipment.

It held eight or ten eggs, depending on egg size, and we achieved quite remarkably high hatch rates with it. It had no fan to circulate the air, and no temperature gauge – a household thermometer had to be inserted through a hole in the side to check that everything was as it should be – but it did the job.

When we bought our own incubator, we also purchased the autoturn cradle, which certainly takes a lot of the worry out of the business of hatching eggs. We found this machine to be very efficient and had good hatch rates, but it has now been superceded by a new model.

If you do end up having to turn eggs by hand, the best way to ensure that you do it evenly is to mark each egg with a big X in pencil on one side. Start them all off with the X facing upwards, then turn them so that the X is face down. Next time, all the X's should be showing again after you have turned them. Turn them either 3 times or 5 times daily. Turning an odd number of times ensures that the eggs lie on alternate sides each night for the long overnight unturned period.

This rather more luxurious incubator has an internal turning mechanism and will hatch up to 42 eggs. It is also available as mains power or 12v DC models. The higher you go up the price range, the more eggs an incubator will hold, and the more refined the operating system becomes.

This larger commercial incubator can hatch 120 hen's eggs at a time. Each level can be fitted with an autoturn mechanism, so that individual trays of eggs can be turned, or not, as required. This particular machine has been in more or less constant use, all year

Turning the eggs is crucial as it keeps the membrane evenly moistened, and more importantly ensures that the membrane passes out toxic waste through the shell.Failure to turn you eggs will result in the contents literally being poisoned.

We eventually bought our own machine, which has an auto-turn cradle that constantly and gradually turns the eggs, is fan-assisted, and has a digital temperature read-out.

There are a wide range of incubators on the market, and as with all things, it's a case of you get what you pay for – the higher the cost, the more bells and whistles that come built in, and the more eggs that they will hold.

Buffy the Wormslayer, our favourite Buff Sussex bantam was convinced that she was a large fowl, and was most unhappy when housed with other bantams. That all changed when we obtained a beautiful cock

Generally speaking, I would say that if you think you will hatch ten eggs at a time, buy an incubator that will hold twenty. It allows for a few duds, and you always end up wanting to hatch more than you originally thought.Remember though that the more eggs you hatch, the more cockerels that you will have to dispose of.

If you eventually upgrade and buy a bigger machine, your original model could be used as a non-turning hatcher by moving the eggs into it when they reach the stage when they should no longer be turned. By carefully recording dates this would enable you to start batches at different times, or hatch large fowl and bantam eggs together.

Running instructions vary slightly from one machine to another, and you should always follow the instructions of the manufacturer. Even so, we found with our incubator that we got slightly better results by adding a bit more water than stated in the instructions, so it's worth experimenting a little if your initial results are disappointing. Humidity and temperature in the room where your incubator is situated will have an effect on the conditions inside the machine, so perhaps the air in the rooms in our centrally heated house is quite dry and that's why we get improved results with more water.

As a general rule, the perfect temperature for hatching eggs is 100°F (37.7°C), but this is at the centre of the egg, for the middle egg in the tray. If your incubator has a fan (forced air type) then the temperature will be constant throughout the egg chamber, and your thermometer should show 37.7°C. In still-air (no fan) incubators the thermometer generally measures the temperature a couple of inches above the eggs, and in this case it should read 103°F (39.4°C) to ensure the correct temperature at egg-level. Remember also that an incubator is designed to be run with a full load for optimum temperature. Running it half-empty is likely to give misleading and inaccurate readings.

Before putting any eggs into your incubator you should set your machine up with the correct level of water included, and then run it for at least 24 hours to make sure that it is working at the correct temperature. If you have to make adjustments then run it for a further day to double check that you've got it right. You should do this every time that you use the incubator, as the settings can sometimes go awry when the machine has been stored.

Whilst running these tests you should bring the eggs into the incubation room in their box to allow them to slowly come up to room temperature, to prevent a sudden rise in temperature when you place them in the incubator to commence incubation. Sudden temperature changes are to

Once you start free ranging chickens in your garden, it is a case of sharing – what is yours is now theirs! Be warned, though, that you will be forever clearing up after them.

By mating a gold gene carrying cockerel with a silver gene hen, the chicks can be sexed at birth. All the light coloured Sussex chicks here are boys, and the darker ones are girls.

The Buff offspring (pullets) can confidently be sold at any age, but the Light Sussex boys should be raised for the table as their genes are impure.

Marital bliss......a lovely picture of a Blue Partridge Wyandotte hen with her Cuckoo Buff Columbian mate, enjoying the freedom of their owner's garden. Chickens can provide a great focal point for your garden, as well as all those lovely fresh eggs. Photo: Cathy Burton

A good strain of Araucana will lay boooooootiful pale blue eggs. The birds are most striking due to their crests, and the whiskers in males. As these are an important point when showing, let's hope that good egg-laying doesn't get sacrificed for show points in future breeding programmes.
Photo: Andy Cawthray

The Leghorn is one of the most prolific traditional breed egg layers, and the large, erect comb of the cock (whilst the female's hangs over one eye) makes them quite distinctive. Leghorns are rather flighty and easily frightened, so their runs should always be covered.
Photo: Cathy Burton

The Brahma is one of the biggest meat birds, yet its great size and fearsome looks are misleading and it is a gentle, friendly bird. Selective show breeding over one hundred years means that 130-140 eggs a year is about what you can expect today, but the cockerels make up for this with their good meat weight.
Photo: Jakki Keeble

If you fancy having lots of lovely, blue-shelled eggs, and chicks that can be sexed at birth, then the Cream Legbar has to be the choice for you. Great care should be taken when purchasing your initial stock as many strains have become tainted and lay olive eggs. Photo: Jakki Keeble

This lovely French Marans is clearly enjoying free-ranging in the garden. Marans are layers of lovely dark brown eggs, if you buy your stock from a good strain. Photo: Rachel Pitt

Welsummers are layers of beautiful dark brown eggs, but again you have to get your birds from good stock. They are inclined to be flighty and adventurous, so need to be housed carefully
Photo: Alison Ingram

The Speckled Sussex was the first colour produced, and all other colours have evolved from it. The beautiful chestnut base colour is supplemented with black and tipped with white, giving the striking spotted effect.
Photo: Jakki Keeble

The Buff Orpington is one of the most popular back garden birds owing to its superb looks and lovely nature. The feather duster look is a great favourite with children, and most keepers aren't concerned that there may be fewer eggs than from other utility breeds. This pretty young pullet will probably grow up to give her owner around 150 or so eggs a year. Photo: Jakki Keeble

The Orpington is one breed that has suffered particularly badly in the utility stakes, in the search for the perfect show bird. The offspring of this beautiful White Orpington cock will lay far fewer eggs than their ancestors of 100 years ago, and he bears little resemblance to his forefathers.

Photo: Julie & Dean Short

Wyandottes come in a superb range of colours, possibly the biggest choice available for any breed. The barred and laced varieties are particularly striking. Lots of eggs, lots of colours, lots of meat and a great bird for beginners – what more could you want from a chicken?
Photo: Cathy Burton

The Light Sussex is probably the most popular of all the utility breeds, so you are never likely to have a problem selling spare birds.

Combining great egg production with excellent carcass size, it is the ideal breed for the smallholder.

Hagrid, our magnificent utility Light Sussex cockerel, had to be given injections, much to his annoyance. Incidentally, there is a saying that goes, "If you are going to roast it, don't name it". We solved this problem by always giving our stock cockerel the same name.
I think that we are now on Hagrid IV

This Blue Laced hen is just one of several colour combinations available in both large fowl and bantam sizes, all of them very beautiful.
Photo: Julie & Dean Short

be avoided at any stage of the hatching process!

You should never incubate different species of birds' eggs in the same batch as hatching requirements are often not compatible. For instance, duck eggs require a higher humidity than chicken eggs.

Similarly, hatching bantams and large fowl at the same time is slightly more complicated as they have different hatching timings, which will make it hard to turn off the autoturn cradle at the correct time. The only way to achieve it is to add any bantam eggs to the incubator two days after the large fowl eggs have started incubating, or operate a separate hatcher as described above.

We incubated one batch once where only one bantam hatched, with several large fowl. We raised them all together and she was convinced she was a large fowl, sulking when we housed her with other bantams. She would sit and pine if placed with other bantams, but brighten up immediately when she was placed back with her huge buddies. She only really finally accepted that she was a bantam when we gave her a bantam boyfriend to keep her happy.

There is nothing stopping you hatching different varieties of large fowl chicken eggs in one go though. Some chick varieties are instantly recognisable as soon as they hatch, but others look similar to one another. If you want to be able to distinguish and separate these ones, then the eggs need to be kept apart from others in the incubator. The easiest way to do this is to place the eggs of one type in a muslin bag in the incubator when you stop turning the eggs. This will ensure good air circulation and warmth - but make sure that it doesn't get caught in the fan!

Once the chicks in the bag hatch and have dried out they

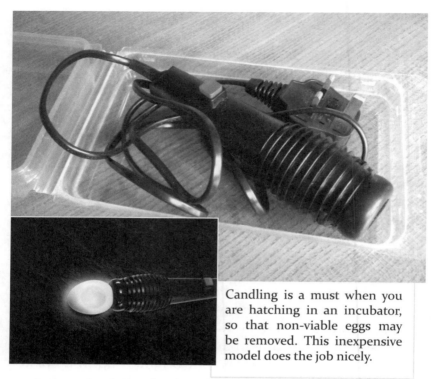

Candling is a must when you are hatching in an incubator, so that non-viable eggs may be removed. This inexpensive model does the job nicely.

can be marked on the head or back with a thick permanent marker pen and all let loose together in your brooder. If there is still a need to identify them when they start to lose their down feathering, they will be big enough for you to fit them with coloured plastic leg rings.

Around 5-7 days into the hatch you should check your eggs for fertility. You do this by a process called 'candling'. This involves passing a bright light through the egg so that you can see the contents. If you are intending to hatch eggs on a regular basis it is worth investing a small amount in a purpose made candler as they are not very expensive. For our first hatches we used a pencil torch with a bright beam with reasonable results.

Early candlers consisted of nothing more than a piece of board with an oval hole cut in it, in which the egg lay, and a light bulb (or candle, hence the name).

The eggs of most breeds can be candled, but the very dark brown eggs of Marans and Welsumers can be very difficult or even impossible to view.

What you are hoping to see at this stage is a filigree of blood vessels inside the egg with a blob at the centre, showing that your future chicks are starting to develop nicely. Incredibly, that tiny blob will contain a heart that has been beating since day three! You will probably find one or two that show nothing at all, and you can see the shape of the yolk. These are infertile and referred to as clear eggs, which should be removed. Sometimes you will see a small, dark smudge, but no blood vessels. These are eggs that have started to develop but then died – this is particularly common in eggs that have been posted and had a rough journey – and they should also be removed.

Eggs that are not developing properly can turn bad very quickly in the heat of an incubator, and as mentioned already, will sometimes burst. The smell is indescribable, and the rotten contents can spread infection through the rest of your hatching eggs, so it is important to remove them as soon as you spot them.

You are also looking to check the size of the air sac at the round end of the egg, as this is an important indicator that you have the humidity at the correct level. If your humidity is too high the air sac will be too small and if it is too low the air sac will be too large.

You should candle again at around 12-14 days, and again remove any eggs that are not developing properly. By this stage you should see very definite development of large blood vessels, and a sizeable chick, which will often react to the bright light with quite sharp movements. There will be a very noticeable air sac.

Three days before the eggs are due to hatch you should stop turning them, and turn off any auto-turn devices. This is to enable the chick to position itself correctly so that it can start the strenuous job of breaking out of the shell. This is the point when the instructions usually tell you to increase the amount of water in the troughs.

From now onwards you could start to hear the young ones cheeping inside the eggs. A sitting hen will "talk" back to them with encouraging noises. This is when things start to get really exciting, and you will probably constantly want to keep peeking to see what's happening. This is fine if your incubator has a transparent top or panel, but don't keep opening it up to inspect the eggs as this will cause dramatic changes to the temperature and humidity – possibly enough to cause the eggs to fail to hatch!

If you follow all the manufacturer's instructions, and are using good-quality fertile eggs, you can reasonably expect an 80% successful hatch rate. If the eggs have been posted to you, the buffeting that they often receive en route means that a 50% hatch can be considered good.

If you are unlucky enough to experience a power cut whilst incubating, there are a few things that you can do. Incubators are designed and built to be fairly well insulated, but if you get a power cut, do everything that you can to increase that insulation by wrapping the machine in blankets or something similar. If the cut lasts longer than an hour or two consider moving the incubator into your airing cupboard or somewhere else similarly warm. As a last resort, place a hot water bottle inside the blankets that you have wrapped around the incubator. Remember that in the wild a bird will often leave its nest for quite some time and all is still well, and that ducks will frequently paddle in cold water before returning to the nest, something which must reduce the temperature of the eggs quite substantially. A power cut isn't necessarily the disaster that it may seem to be.

Whilst mentioning disasters, how about this one? I dropped eggs that I was candling at 14 days and cracked several of them! I managed to save them by painting over the cracks with a layer of clear nail varnish (my wife's, not mine) which effectively stopped the egg contents from evaporating, and prevented infection from entering. The eggs hatched out just fine. Chicken embryos are clearly tougher little critters than we think they are.

There are various reasons why eggs don't reach the hatching stage, and this seems an appropriate time to list the main ones:

Clear Eggs

The are infertile. This could be because you tried mating too early in the season and the cockerel hadn't reached fertility, he could be too old (or too young), or you could have him with too many females so that he can't fertilise them all. Have you fed him correctly – is he too fat? Have the hens got very fluffy vents so that mating is unsuccessful? The eggs may be too old, or may have been handled roughly – this particularly applies to posted eggs.

Died Early

Candling shows a ring of blood, a smudge of something, or a small embryo where the egg has started to develop. Again, rough handling can cause this to happen. It may also be due to temperatures being too high or too low or fluctuating wildly. It may also be that the eggs are infected with germs that penetrated the shell, or even viruses inherited from parents.

Hatched Early

Chicks hatch out before you expect them (mark your calendar with the expected date) and often have bloody rear ends. This is caused, quite simply, by the temperature being too high.

Unabsorbed Yolks

The chicks are born without absorbing the remaining yolks and die quickly. This is uncommon, but can be caused by low humidity, temperature fluctuations, or possibly by not turning the eggs at regular intervals.

Deformed chicks

This is almost always the result of too much inbreeding in the parent stock – breeding from birds that are too closely related. Twisted feet may be caused by too high a temperature. Deformed chicks can sometimes be quite horrifyingly wrong. All should be immediately and humanely destroyed. If you select unrelated parents, and give them a good balanced diet, you are unlikely to experience deformed young.

Dead in Shell

If the eggs have pipped but then failed to hatch it is almost certainly down to low humidity or high temperature. The

Hatching can be spread out over a couple of days. Here, one chick has already emerged and some eggs are pipping, whilst most show no signs of hatching as yet.

chicks have tried to get out but failed as the membrane dried out too quickly.

Hopefully your good management will have prevented any of these problems and your eggs will now begin to 'pip' (small holes appearing) and move around and wobble. This is quite amusing to watch, and is caused by the struggles of the chick inside, trying to get into position. At this point you should check the water in the troughs and fill it to maximum, as the eggs are now entering the danger period when the membrane can dry out and become leathery.

One important point is that you should always top up with warm water. Opening up the incubator will have already lost all the warm air, and if you fill up with cold water it will take much longer for the machine to get back to the

One morning you will come downstairs and this is the sight that is likely to greet you. Remove the egg shells, pop the chicks that have dried out into your brooder (which of course you will have set up ready, won't you? Yeah, right.) and leave the freshly hatched wet ones in the incubator. Place the lid back on the incubator and leave well alone for a few more hours.

It is best to remove the dry active chicks because they will keep climbing over the eggs that are still hatching, and disturbing them.

correct incubation temperature, as the cold water will have to be heated as well as the cold air. The change in temperature could kill or stunt the growth of your developing embryos.

Don't get over-excited when the first holes appear as it can still take up to 24 hours for them to hatch – this is a long and laborious job for the chick, and they will take frequent long rests in between spells of chipping away at the shell. They will, however, gradually cut their way right round the circumference of the shell, and then, with one final heave, shove the end off and burst out into the world.....

and promptly collapse with exhaustion.

The chances are that most of this will have happened during the dead of night, when you were snoring away upstairs, and the first that you will know of it is when you enter the room and switch on the light.

Instantly, all the newly-hatched chicks will bounce upright and cheep for attention and food from you, their surrogate mother. Other than removing the shells from hatched eggs you should do nothing. The chicks need to rest and regain their strength, and more importantly dry out so that their down feathering fluffs up to keep them warm. It is important to remove the hatched shells as they can very easily cup the end of another egg that is still to hatch, imprisoning the chick inside.

Don't worry about them starving to death as they can comfortably live off the contents of the yolk, which has been ingested into their abdomens, for the first few hours of their lives.

When you see that some of the chicks are alert and dry, you can then remove them to your brooder box. There are all sorts of elaborate bits and pieces that you can buy, including heat lamps with special elements, and complete heated brooders. Although we have used them in the past we don't bother now as we have a much simpler method, and our chicks generally only need to use it for around 12 hours.

Our brooder consists of a large plastic storage box with folding half lids, of the type that you can buy in many large stores and supermarkets. We line the floor with a section of corrugated cardboard from a roll, with the crinkly side uppermost, but you could also use an old towel or something similar. It is needed because the floor of the box is smooth and slippery, and the chicks could get splayed feet if they slide around. Over this we position the lamp head of an old anglepoise lamp, which we bought for the purpose, leaving about a two-inch gap. We replaced the standard bulb with a 60w red bulb intended for use inside electric fires to give a flame effect. Finally we place a couple of water containers inside the box, consisting of shallow jam jar lids. If we use deeper containers for larger broods we place small stones inside and fill to their level with water. Finally, we liberally scatter chick crumbs around on the floor. If we have hatched a particularly large brood we will use a second lamp to give a bigger heated area.

Chicks instinctively peck at anything around them, and scattering crumbs loose on the floor gets them feeding very quickly and recognising what is food. By day two the crumbs can be placed in a bowl or small hopper. If you notice that a chick really doesn't know what to do, try tapping at pieces of crumb next to the chick with your finger, or picking a crumb up and dropping it in front of the chick. This mimics the actions of a parent bird and will often stimulate the chick into pecking. You are rarely likely to encounter this problem unless you are unlucky enough to get only a single egg hatch, or one hatches very late and its siblings have already moved onto the next stage. Generally, as soon as one chick is pecking at crumbs, the rest will follow suit.

Three important points to make here; the reason that we fill the larger pots with stones is because new born chicks are extremely weak and fragile. They have short bursts of activity, and then collapse with exhaustion. If they happen to collapse into a water dish, they will simply drown. The pebbles prevent this from happening. We actually use healing crystals in our water pots, which causes amusement with people who see them. The simple truth is that they are the ideal size – and who knows, they might just give the chicks

A mixed batch of Sussex and Wyandotte bantams enjoy a well earned rest after the exertions of chasing each other around. Wyandottes are not just beautiful as adults, the chicks are equally attractive.

that little bit of extra strength that they need.

The second important point to make is that this system only works because our chicks are already somewhat recovered and active before we place them in our brooder box. Newly hatched chicks would stagger under the lamps, collapse...... and cook! Instead, they move out a bit if it is too hot, and form a ring around the lamp – if this happens, raise the lamp fractionally. If the lamp is too high the chicks will huddle together under it to keep warm - lower it a fraction.

Large commercial operations hatch their eggs in darkness and a light attracts the newly-hatched chicks to one end, where they promptly slide down a chute and land in the brooder area. This section is heated evenly throughout with a gentle heat so that there is no danger of frying the young.

Lastly, we change the normal white bulb to a red one because this helps to stop the chicks attacking each other!

Small pebbles placed in the drinking dishes help to prevent small chicks from drowning. They are only needed for the first day or two after hatching, when the chicks are still weak after their exertions to

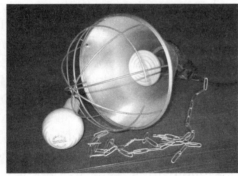

Here our livestock heat lamp has had the standard infrared bulb replaced with a 60w dull emitter bulb. The more powerful 150w emitter can be used with bigger hatches in bigger spaces. Note the hanging chain, which allows the lamp height to be adjusted accurately

Chickens are pretty horrible creatures really and will peck at anything bloody or red, and this could well be the red, raw rear end of a newly hatched chick. They will literally peck them to death. A red bulb not only reduces the glare, but helps to disguise any minor wounds by making them appear black.

If we are using a broody

It doesn't take long for chicks to outgrow the "oh aren't they lovely" stage. Care has to taken with keeping them warm at this halfway house between fluffy down and full plumage stage.

foster mother the chicks are only kept in our broody box for the first day, and that evening they are transferred under the sitting hen, as mentioned previously. If no hen is available, then we will grow them on in the box for a week or so, until their adult feathering is beginning to come through. We then move them on into a much larger box and use a commercial heat lamp to take them on to the next stage. Do not use a heat lamp over a small box – the chicks will have no way of moving away if they get too hot.

Heat lamps are available from just about any farm supply shop, as they are used to keep various young livestock warm. Don't use the infra red bulb supplied with it, but buy a dull emitter type separately. Your local shops are unlikely to stock them as they are rather specialist, but they may be able to order you one, or alternatively you can easily buy one by mail order or online. They are available in wattages from 60w to 250w.

They have two main advantages over infra red bulbs, the first being that they give off no light, which is wasted energy and also keeps the chicks active 24 hours a day and may damage their eyes. When we used a standard infra red bulb in the brooder in our garden shed at night the shed appeared to be on fire!

The other advantage of a dull emitter bulb is that, if handled carefully, they virtually last forever and seldom burn out in operation – an important factor if you keep your chicks in a shed or outhouse on a bitterly cold night when a blown bulb can mean death for them all.

The grower box doesn't have to be anything fancy. We use a simple homemade one constructed from plywood which is four feet long by two feet high and two feet wide, and has a removable wire lid.

This is stood on a table in our garden shed in front of the window, and the heat lamp hung overhead. At first the lamp is hung very low, an inch or so above the wire cover, but as the birds grow and their plumage develops this is gradually raised to reduce the amount of heat given and to harden the chicks off.

Wattages of the lamps/emitters vary, so the safest way to get it right is to place a thermometer in your box, under the lamp, and adjust the height of the lamp until the temperature reads 90°F (32°C), and this is perfect for newly hatched chicks. The temperature should then be reduced by five degrees each week by raising the lamp until it is down to around 65°F (18°C). The lamps generally come supplied with a hanging chain, so adjusting the height is simple. After a few weeks

This home made house cost me just £40 in materials in 2005. The run has two lifting roof sections, and the house roof is also on hinges to allow access. It makes an excellent grower run and broody box combined. For the first two weeks after hatching the chicks are confined in the house section by a wire grill over the entrance, which allows light in but keeps them safe. If I were building it again I would include a door in the side of the run so that the chickens can be let out into the garden, and I would probably attach wire over the whole of the run floor to keep out vermin.

they will only need the lamp at night, and once they are fully feathered it is no longer necessary.

If you are growing chicks on in warm weather, be sure to check up on them regularly, and if need be, leave the shed door open to increase ventilation. We nearly lost a whole batch from heat stroke when the sun suddenly burst through on a dull day. We returned home to find all the chicks collapsed. Only swift action, placing them in front of a cool fan and trickling cold water down their throats, saved the day and reduced casualties to just a couple that were too far gone.

This Buff Sussex bantam chick is almost certainly a male as the feathers on its back are growing slower than the rest of the plumage.

You should never try to keep your young stock indoors beyond the first couple of weeks, as the amount of dust they create has to be seen to be believed!

Whether your chicks are raised by a foster mum or under heat lamps, by the time they are eight weeks old or so it will be time to move them on to the next stage of their growth. If they are with a foster hen, she will have had enough by now, and will want to start laying again. She will drive the chicks away from her and peck at them, much to their dismay and bewilderment.

At this point we move the chicks to their own run, combining

This Wyandotte bantam chick is exactly the same age as the Sussex in the picture above, and came from the same hatch. It is probably a pullet as the feathering is much more even.

all the chicks of similar ages. They have a full-sized run and their own 4´ x 4´ shed with a hay or straw covered floor so that they can huddle together and keep warm on chilly nights. The feeder and drinker are slightly raised off the floor, but there are no roosting perches – the chicks all nestle down together at night. Chickens should not be given perches until they are at least ten weeks old as they can permanently damage their feet if used earlier. If it is a particularly frosty day it is better to leave them shut in the house when they are very young.

Do not put chicks of different ages together at any stage, as the older chicks will bully the younger ones and peck them quite badly, possibly even killing them. If they are under six weeks old, age mixes should not be different by more than a week. From six weeks to twelve weeks you can probably stretch this to a couple of week's age difference.

It is at around the eight week stage that you can really begin to judge what sex the youngsters are. Young cocks will have a more upright stance, longer, sturdier legs and their combs will have begun developing. They will also have started behaving like the obnoxious bullies that they are!

Females will have a slightly 'flatter' carriage, and their tails usually develop before those of the boys. There are ways of sexing them much earlier – from the moment that they are born, in fact – but it takes a lot of experience. Day-old chicks can be vent sexed by an expert, which involves a careful observation of their rear end and sexual organs. I have tried it, having carefully studied pictures in books......and given up! There are far too many variations for each sex, and some of them are virtually identical. I'll leave it to the experts.

There are some early signs that you can watch out for though, when the chicks first start to feather up. Those that show the earliest signs of feathering are almost certainly females, and they also tend to grow their stubby tails first, usually at around three weeks old. Another technique is to spread out their wings and take a look at the first few wing feathers; the primary flight feathers. The females grow these feathers faster, so they will stand out further than those of the males.

When they are slightly older, the ones that still have bald backs are more likely to be male. Have a go at sexing them at various stages and make a note of your results, then check them later when the birds reach around twelve weeks and can be sexed more easily – but bear in mind that even then you can be wrong, when one that you thought was a hen starts crowing.

We separate our cockerels and pullets into separate pens when they are around 12 weeks old so that the hens can be switched to layers' pellets whilst the boys continue on growers'/finishing pellets to get them to a good size for the oven. It also helps to cut down the fights between the unruly boys, and will quickly show you if you have made a mistake sexing any of your stock.

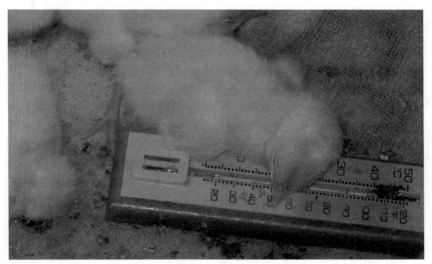

Chapter Six

Culling

This is the difficult part. I am going to give you some quite gory details in this section, so be prepared. If you find it unpleasant to read about it, then quite honestly you are unlikely to be able to do it, and you should perhaps be reconsidering whether you can raise chickens to supply your own meat. It isn't pleasant killing them after you have put so much love and care into raising them, and it doesn't really get any easier as time goes by and you build up experience, although you do perhaps harden yourself to it.

Depending on the breed, you can begin enjoying wonderfully tasty roast dinners from about five months old. We generally consider six months to be about the optimum age for our Sussex. Up until then they tend to be boney and lanky, but then suddenly fill out. Much beyond six months and the meat begins to be rather tough.

Remove the feeders the night before culling is to take place, as dressing the carcass will be easier when the crop is empty, but leave them with water.

One important point to make is that your Sunday roast should be killed out of sight and sound of the rest of your chickens.

I tried many times to kill chickens by the conventional hand neck-breaking method, and although I had a limited success with bantams, I simply couldn't master it with large fowl, which have much tougher necks. I studied pictures and instructions in books, and just couldn't get the knack of it, even though I am 6'6" tall and very strong. I eventually enlisted the help of an experienced chicken keeper, who showed me the technique at first hand.

Sadly, it is the chicken that suffers if things don't go to plan. As the whole point of raising your chickens is to give them a good life, free from stress and cruelty, you really can't afford to make a hash of it at this crucial stage. I am not even going to attempt to give you a verbal or pictorial guide to wringing their necks in this book, that's how strongly I feel about it. In the early days we once 'killed' a large Buff Sussex cockerel by this method, only to have him wake up while we were plucking him, and I would hate for you to have the same experience!

I will, however, tell you how I have got on with various other methods, and also how some of my friends have coped with this awkward problem.

One of the oldest ways of killing poultry is the broomstick method. If you hold a chicken down on the ground it is quite easy to lay its neck flat. You then place a broom handle across its neck and stand lightly on each end. Holding onto its feet you then stand up straight, apply your full weight to your feet, and yank on the legs. This very effectively dislocates the bird's neck and death is considered to be instantaneous.

However, with a big bird it isn't always easy to tell that you have done it, and so you invariably yank some more to make sure that you've finished the job, and this almost always results in the head being pulled off.

The phrase 'running around like a headless chicken' is firmly based on fact. Remove its head and a chicken will still flap around and get quite a distance, spraying blood in all directions from its severed neck. The head will often continue to open and close its beak and blink its eyes. The body movements are all just nerve reactions as the animal is quite dead and minus its head, but it takes some getting used to. It is also rather messy.

It is probably a good idea to witness somebody else culling a chicken at least once so that you see it and believe it, as whichever method you choose to kill your bird, they will still continue to flap around. It is hard to believe that they are actually dead, and for this reason you need to choose a method where you know that they are dead, rather than feeling the need to keep killing them repeatedly. This is time-consuming for you and rather tedious for the dead bird!

Another time-honoured method is to chop their heads off with an axe. I've never tried it myself – it was hard enough getting the blood off my trousers after trying the broomstick method, so I don't fancy getting my shirt drenched too. A friend of mine has, however, refined this technique somewhat, and swears by the method. He has ground the cutting edge off a hand axe to make it completely blunt. He lays the bird on the ground so that its neck is stretched across something solid like a log, and whacks its neck with the blunt axe. It breaks the neck as clean as a whistle and makes no mess at all.

The 'in' way to kill your bird at the moment is using a humane dispatcher. Hand-held versions of these are available, and some are little more than a glorified pair of pliers. I really don't understand why they are so expensive. Mine came with no instructions, and friends have said theirs were the same, which is rather appalling. It is essential to brush the neck feathers forward so that the tool can be used on bare skin, and it should be applied as high on the neck as possible, at the narrowest point. It works reasonably satisfactorily on bantams, but is not totally effective on large fowl, and is likely to end up just being a weapon of strangulation. I have learned to use mine by squeezing hard on the tool and then jerking it sharply. This action crushes the vertebrae and snaps the neck at the same instant, and seems to render them instantly unconscious.

A system that seems to be much more effective is using a wall-mounted humane dispatcher. These are a bit more expensive than the hand held models, but seem to be more efficient. They have a screw fitting that adjusts the gap between the jaws, and this has to be set to as small as possible to ensure that the bird's neck is dislocated and broken, but not so narrow that it actually decapitates when operated. Friends tell me that this type of dispatcher is easy for one person to use unaided, and doesn't need huge strength applied to the handle. It is easy enough to hold the bird under one arm, use your free hand to place its neck in the jaws and then operate the handle.

And finally......you could of course get somebody else to do the job for you – but that would be cowardly, wouldn't it?

Whichever method you choose, you should be aware that there is a good chance that legislation is likely to change in the near future. The organisation "Compassion in World Farming" are campaigning vigorously for the sale of humane dispatchers to be banned as they claim that the bird still experiences pain. Similarly, they allege that decapitation is no answer as the head continues to live for around twenty seconds after being severed – I must admit that my own experiences tend to substantiate this. They want all livestock killed by stunning first, and then throat cutting, which is all well and good, but stunning equipment is very expensive and not really viable for the backyard chicken keeper.

There does, however, seem to be an acceptance by all parties that the traditional hand neck-breaking both stuns and kills at the same time, so the conclusion has to be that you should find somebody who can teach you the way to cull your stock by hand before even considering raising poultry for the table.

Chapter Seven
Oven Ready

Plucking

You still have work to do once you have killed your dinner, and the first step is plucking the bird. The quicker you start plucking, the easier it will be.

The first point is that if the bird is more than six months old, it probably isn't even worth plucking it, as the meat will be too tough to roast. However, all is not lost, as an older bird will casserole wonderfully. You don't need to go to the trouble of plucking though, as it is much easier to skin the carcass, complete with feathers.

We only use the breast, thigh and leg meat from older chickens.

We have found it easiest to hold the carcass inside an empty feed bag and pluck it there so that all the loose feathers are held inside the bag. If you hang the bird by one leg it is quite convenient to work on, but the slightest breeze and you will find yourself (and your garden) surrounded by a whirling mass of feathers.

All the books tell you to start with the most difficult feathers – the wing flight feathers, and tail – when plucking, as these will become harder still to get out as the bird cools down. Certainly you should pull the tail feathers out, but a butcher friend gave us a tip about the flight feathers, and now we don't remove them until we are dressing the bird for the oven. At that stage, and with the bird cold, it is easy to simply cut a slit along the back edge of the wing beside the feathers

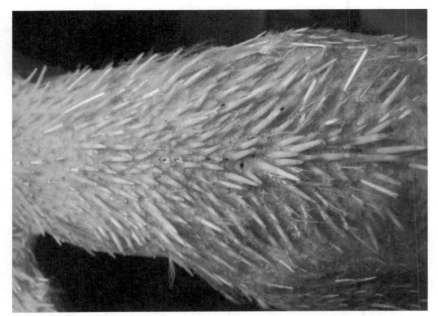

If killing an older bird, try not to do it during the annual moult. If you do have to you will find when you pluck it that beneath the plumage are hundreds of pinfeathers – new feathers waiting to come through to replace the old feathers as they are dropped. They are very fiddly and tedious to remove. We personally don't bother as we only use meat from the breast, thighs and legs of older birds. You will not encounter this problem when killing younger birds as they do not moult until their second autumn.

and pull them out cleanly.

Having removed the tail feathers, you should then pluck the legs and work your way forward, plucking in the direction that the feathers grow, rather than against them. This will avoid tearing the skin.

When you reach the breast area it is a good idea to press the thumb of your free hand against the skin at the base of the feather as you pull with the other hand, as the breast skin is particularly easy to tear.

Don't be too fussy, trying to remove every tiny piece of feather or hair.

You may find that you killed the bird at the start of the moult, and the fluffy under feathers are full of tiny young new feathers (pin feathers) coming through. These are very fiddly to get out, and come free easier after the bird has been hung and is cold. When you are preparing the bird for the oven, the last thing that you will do is singe it with a naked flame to remove anything that is left.

Hanging

No, we aren't making doubly sure that the bird is dead! Hanging is the traditional next stage of preparing your bird for cooking. It consists of merely suspending the bird by its legs somewhere cool and away from flies. This allows the blood to drain into the broken neck cavity to give nice white meat, and improves the flavour. The longer you hang the bird, the stronger the flavour will become, becoming really "gamey" if left too long. We prefer a nice delicate flavour, and so kill our birds and pluck them in the morning one day, hang them overnight, then dress them the following evening.

Dressing

Isn't that a most peculiar expression – dressing the bird? Having stripped it stark naked of feathers, you then dress it!

It refers, of course, to the final part of the process – removing all the parts of the carcass that you don't want to cook. Some people find the killing to be the worst part of raising your own chickens for meat, but I beg to differ – removing the innards is far worse. It is a messy and smelly job, and

A dead chicken is not a pretty sight. Killing one is not pleasant, and hanging the bird drains the blood into the head and neck giving it a bright red swollen look. Notice that some pinfeathers remain.

The more eagle eyed will have noticed that the wing tips have already been removed from the carcass pictured above. The wing tips and feathers can be removed in one action.

the longer that you have hung the bird, the worse the smell is! I have large hands, which make the job doubly difficult as you have to insert your whole hand inside the body cavity to pull out the bulk of the innards, which by then are stone cold and feel awful.

The first job, however, is to remove the wingtips. The feathers at the very tip are often very difficult to pull out. It is much simpler to chop them off. If you look closely you will notice a patch of white gristle about one inch from the wingtip. Chopping through this point, and then cutting down along the back of the wing, removes these feathers easily.

Cutting the skin just below the knee, around the front and sides, the leg can then be broken by rapping it sharply.

The next stage is to take off the feet, and as part of the process pull out tendons. To do this you cut the skin just below the knee around the front and both sides, but not at the back. You then position the leg out over the edge of your work surface and strike it sharply, breaking the leg.

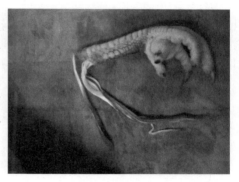

You now have to pull the broken leg very hard to pull the tendon out from the back of the leg. This isn't at all a simple job and I find it easier to twist the broken section of bone round and round, effectively twisting

It will be a struggle, but pulling the leg tendons out will help to tenderise the meat. This isn't done with commercial chickens, but they haven't had six months of running around to build up their muscles!

the tendon tighter and tighter on itself, and then give a long steady pull. Be careful as it breaks suddenly, and you can end up in a heap on the floor. You can then cut away the remaining piece of shinbone, taking it back to the knuckle of the knee.

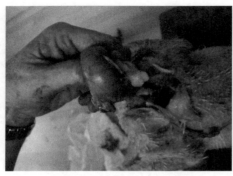

This bird has not had the feed removed the night before, and so its crop is full. Care should be taken not to split it as removing it then

My butcher friend says that you don't have to go through this performance and can simply cut the legs off. He is used to dealing with very young birds though – five or six weeks old – that haven't had much exercise and so haven't fully developed these tendons.

Take care not to cut too deeply, as severing the intestines will make the next stage more unpleasant.

We on the other hand are dealing with a six month old rooster who has been strutting his stuff with the girls, roosting, and running around, all of which activities strength the muscles and tendons, and so we prefer to remove them.

The next stage is to remove the head and neck, which is the messiest part of the job as the blood will have collected in the neck during hanging. We cut the head off at the point where the neck is broken, peel the neck skin back as far as possible, and force the neck backwards over the body, which breaks the neck at the shoulder point. Cut the flesh all round and remove the neck.

Split the neck skin down to the breastbone and remove the crop.

The next job is to carefully cut all round the anus, taking great care not to cut too deeply and so sever the intestines. Pinch the flesh at the base of the breast bone and cut across half way between there and the anus. From the ends of the first incision, cut to either side of the anus.

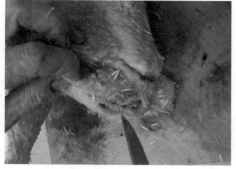

Cut down to the parson's nose, just breaking through into the stomach

Finally, cut across at the base of the parson's nose, creating a hole big enough to be able to insert your hand into the body cavity.

The final cut releases the anus so that the innards can he removed.

The final cut releases the anus so that the innards can be removed.

You can now pull away the severed anus and surrounding skin, and the intestines will follow with it. Do not pull them too hard, or they will snap and spill their contents inside the carcass. Reach inside the cavity, run your fingers all round the cavity, releasing anything attached, take a firm grip on the innards and pull steadily – most of them should come out in one piece.

The stomach wall can be carefully split lengthwise until you reach the lining, and this can be removed with its contents. The stomach wall, together with the neck and liver, can serve as a very tasty ingredient of your gravy stock.

Pulled steadily, but firmly, all the entrails should come out in one go. Notice that this bird has had too much corn as the stomach to the right has a thick layer of fat around it. As the hen was moulting there were no immature eggs to contend with.

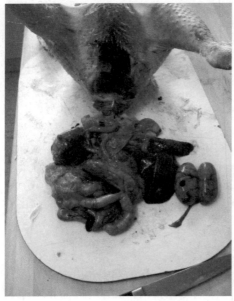

Compare this picture to the one above. The large testicles are to the right of the picture. This bird was clearly a dominant rooster!

If the bird is a cockerel, I can promise you that he'll surprise you with the size of his testicles! In proportion to its body size, they are massive. Interestingly, when we have butchered young cockerels that have lived in the shadow of a large adult cock, their testicles have been much smaller, and in the really aggressive boys they are huge. Clearly, testosterone levels affect masculinity.

Apparently in the East they are eaten, but I've never fancied the idea personally.

On the other hand, if the bird is a laying female, then the job will be somewhat messier as you will be pulling several semi-developed eggs out with the innards.

The innards should always be handled carefully as you remove them, as tucked away inside them all will be the gall bladder, and if this bursts and spills its contents on the flesh, it will be ruined and inedible as the bile is incredibly bitter.

Other organs such as heart, liver and kidneys will probably come free with the main clump of innards, but if not they can be picked out easily if you want to use them in your stock. The gall bladder will be attached to the liver, and should be trimmed off very carefully, removing a piece of liver rather than cutting the bladder.

The legs can be secured ready for roasting by making cuts in the stomach and tucking the legs through them.

Alternatively, tie string around the parson's nose, bring the ends over the legs and knot securely, trimming away any excess string.

The only parts remaining will be the lungs – bright red organs stuck to the inside of the ribs. It is a matter of choice whether you leave them or remove them. They can be removed by digging a finger in behind them, or using the tip of a sharp knife, or there is even a special tool available for this tricky job.

You should now thoroughly flesh the body cavity out with cold water.

The next job is to singe the carcass with a burning spill to clean off any remaining hairs and feather stubble, and wash it with cold water, drying it off with kitchen towel.

As the bird that was slaughtered was an old girl, we will not be roasting
her, but she will be casseroled as per our recipe later in the book. Both
sides of the breast are skinned and trimmed away from the ribs, and
the legs and thighs are removed and skinned. The liver, heart and

The last part of the oven ready process is to secure the legs,
either by making two cuts in the stomach and tucking the
legs in them, or by tying the knuckles to the parson's nose.

I should just again mention here that, although the flesh of
your home raised chicken will be tender and tasty, its skin
will be tough. We always remove the cooked skin before
carving the bird to serve for dinner. You have to remember
that a shop-bought chicken is likely to be only 5 weeks old,
and its skin will still be soft and tender – not so with a six
month old bird that has been running around in your garden
or allotment.

Chapter Eight
Problems

This section is not going to be a complete dictionary of poultry ailments – there have been complete books written on that topic.

My aim is merely to give you hints and tips on the sort of problems that you are most likely to encounter as a newcomer – in other words, many of the things that happened to us!

Chickens, as I have said several times already, are not very nice to each other. If a bird is poorly, and shows it, the others will pick on it, often pecking it to death. Because of this, sick birds try to conceal the fact that they are ill. By the time that a chicken looks sufficiently ill for you to notice, believe me it is really ill. Although there are now many vets that are accustomed to treating poultry because of the large increase in the number of people that keep them as garden pets, consultations and medicines are not cheap.

In the past we have obtained treatment for favourite birds, but now we simply cull sick birds quickly and humanely. As our birds are rarely over two years old, and we don't buy in outside stock (thus risking bringing in infection), we rarely have to resort to this measure.

The important thing is to observe your birds carefully whenever you are around them and be aware of any untypical behaviour. Anything sitting around hunched up or with fluffed up feathers isn't feeling one hundred percent. Keep an eye on droppings – loose, green or liquid smelly droppings are often the first signs of major problems.

Your birds should be alert, active, and interested in what

you are doing around them. Any bird under the weather should be removed immediately from a communal run and placed in isolation.

Soft Shelled Eggs

You may occasionally find that you get eggs that are soft shelled, or indeed have no shell at all. When a pullet comes into lay for the first time, her first few eggs may be soft shelled, and this isn't anything to worry about; her egg-laying system just hasn't fully kicked in yet.

You may, incidentally, find that her first egg is the size of a marble, which always makes us smile, especially when she has sat around all day looking uncomfortable. So much effort for so little reward!

If you encounter soft shelled eggs at other times, you need to act quickly. Chickens love nothing better than a nice, tasty egg, and once they have developed a taste for them it can lead to problems with persistent egg eating. If the shells are soft the hens are not getting enough calcium in their diet, either due to a shortage of grit availability or because they are not eating it. Offer the birds wet mash, and mix grit and oyster shell or crushed egg shells in with it.

If the problem persists, and you can identify the offender, it may be necessary to cull her. If the other birds start eating their eggs it can sometimes become a habit that is almost impossible to prevent.

Persistent Broodies

Some hens are determined to raise young, no matter what the odds. If you find that a hen (or often, hens) is in the nest box every time you check it, and scuttles back the instant your back is turned after you have turfed her out, then you need to break her of the habit. If you do not currently need a broody she is effectively useless, as she will not be laying whilst broody. This is particularly likely to be a problem in late summer. Often the simplest method is to move her to another house that doesn't have a nestbox. The changed surroundings are often enough to restore her interest in day to day living, and forget about sitting.

Unfortunately, if she is really determined, this won't do the trick, and she will hunker down in a corner somewhere and stare at you defiantly. At this point you must place her in a

An all-wire cage like this is absolutely ideal for breaking a persistent broody, as the flow of air under the wire floor will cool her breast down. Food and water containers should be hung inside the cage, and don't forget that this cage offers no protection from sun or rain, so should be placed in a sheltered spot.

cage with a raised wire floor, so that air can circulate around her and cool her overheated breast down. She should be given food and water and left for a day or two in a shady, dry spot. This usually does the trick.

Red Mite

These are one of the first major problems that you are likely to encounter, and their effects may be catastrophic without your even knowing that you have a problem. Unlike other mites, red mite do not live on their hosts. Indeed, they may even be living several feet away during the daytime – under the roofing felt is a favourite hiding place. As darkness falls they make their way to the roosting or sitting birds and reveal their Dracula tendencies by sucking the birds' blood.

Red mite can survive for a long time – several weeks in fact – between feeds. When they haven't fed for a while they are tiny, grey, almost transparent specks, but when they have gorged themselves on your precious birds' blood they swell up and are bright red. A bad infestation will literally suck so much blood that their victims will weaken and die very rapidly.

They don't like cold damp weather, and are at their worst during a hot dry summer, so poultry keepers shouldn't complain when we get a terrible summer as the red mite are far less of a problem then – every cloud has a silver lining.

Giveaway signs include specks of blood on eggs and also possibly on the birds' plumage, eggs being laid on the floor because the birds don't want to enter the infested nest boxes, pale combs and pale egg yolks - the latter symptoms both due to anaemia.

Red mite are a troublesome scourge that can prove very difficult to shift once established. This colony is surrounded by the grey detritus of old eggs, shed skins and excreta. The tiny white mites are newly hatched young that haven't yet gorged on the blood of my chickens to make them turn into the fat red monsters that are the older mites. These were discovered on the underside of a droppings shelf and quickly disposed of!

You should regularly check inside your hen house, removing any perches, lids, doors etc. to check behind them because these little perishers hide in every nook and cranny. They lie up in colonies that form a solid clump.

I have had them colonise the door jamb of the main entrance door to my shed. As I opened the door each morning they showered down on me. To the best of my knowledge they don't bite humans, but their scuttling around on the surface of the skin drives you mad. One of my chicken-keeping neighbours on the allotments complained about a constant itching. I told him he had red mite. He didn't believe me, so I took a look at his arm and soon spotted some crawling around. His eyesight wasn't too good and so he had missed them.

There are proprietary red mite powders available, but they are fairly expensive and I'm not convinced as to their effectiveness. It may be that regular use will prevent an outbreak, but certainly once you have a bad infestation the ones that I have tried don't do very much.

Similarly, something new entered the market two or three years ago, claiming to be the cure-all for virtually everything. It revels in the exotic name of diatomaceous Earth and consists of the shells of tiny fossilised creatures (diatoms), whose skeletons are microscopically spiky and sharp. The theory is that pests like mites can't pass through or over it without having their protective skins pierced by the sharp points, causing them to dry out and die. A lot of poultry keepers seem to swear by the stuff, but personally I never had much luck with it. Perhaps I didn't use enough of it, as it is fairly expensive and I probably spread it around too thinly.

I also used it as a panic measure when we were overwhelmed by red mite – perhaps the little terrors were able to crawl over the knee deep dead bodies of their kin and remained untouched!

In cases of severe infestation I have found only one thing works – shut the hens out in the run and spray absolutely every internal surface, nook, cranny and crack thoroughly with a fairly strong, diluted solution of Jeyes Fluid. You can almost hear the little blighters scream as it catches them.

Leave the doors and vents open to aid drying for a couple of hours or so, and then spread wood shavings around to absorb any remaining dampness, before letting the birds back indoors.

Northern Fowl Mite

Nowhere near as damaging as red mite, this grey variety live on their hosts. I think most domesticated poultry, and indeed nearly all wild birds, carry some. The best way to check your stock is to pick up one of your birds, gently turn it upside down, and have a rummage in the fluffy feathers around the vent area, carefully looking at the exposed skin around the feather bases. Little grey things crawling around are the enemy. Fortunately these ones are nowhere near as hard to get rid of – a thorough dusting of the birds and the nest boxes with louse powder usually does the trick.

Scaly leg

This disfiguring malady is caused by yet another mite, which burrows under the scales on the bird's legs, eventually causing them to lift and look awful. It becomes very painful for the poor affected bird to walk. Do not, under any circumstances, try to pick off the stoney-looking secretions. These are actually solidified mite excreta, and the scales will come off in chunks, sometimes taking the flesh off down to the bone. This problem is highly contagious. Under no circumstances use a broody that has scaly leg to incubate eggs as all the chicks will become affected. The treatment that we have found works very well is to dip the legs in surgical spirit twice a week, and then smear them with Vaseline jelly. Do this for three weeks and the mites and any eggs will be killed, and the crust will gradually soften and drop off. Eventually, when the bird moults, the damaged scales will be shed and all will be fine.

Crop Bound

The indications of this malady are a large, hard bulge at the bird's throat, a loss of appetite and possibly the bird gaping and stretching in an attempt to clear its throat. It is caused by eating long grass or tough stalks whole, which get stuck in the crop and then trap further food, causing a build-up and blockage. The bird can no longer feed with a blocked crop, and will eventually starve to death. Gentle massage or the administration of a little olive oil down the throat will sometimes clear the problem, but it is best not to try this until somebody who knows what they are doing has shown you the technique. The best cure is prevention. If you are allowing your chickens onto grass it is much better to keep it cut short so that they can only peck off and eat short pieces, and don't feed them the clippings. The crop is a holding area for freshly eaten food, which is then passed down to the gizzard, where it is ground up with grit by muscular contractions. If the blockage has reached down to the gizzard it is likely to prove fatal. I have heard of the gizzard being opened, the blockage removed and then stitched up by a vet, but this is likely to be extremely expensive.

Egg Bound

This causes a large bulge at the other end of the bird! The vent will be swollen and distended, possibly even prolapsed where part of the oviduct is sticking from the vent. The bird will be most unhappy, sitting around fluffed up, often straining to clear the blockage.

Is it surprising that our poor hens sometimes get egg bound? Double yolker eggs are often nearly twice the size of normal ones, and are bound to make the chooks' eyes water somewhat!

It can be caused by an overly large egg, possibly a double yolker where two eggs have been held up in the system and one shell has formed around them, or by the bird simply being too fat. The bird sits around waiting to die, and usually this is what happens. The situation can sometimes be resolved by bathing the vent, applying a lubricant and leaving the bird in a warm room, but in all honesty, if a proloapse has occurred then it is very likely to happen again in the future and it is more humane to cull.

Coccidiosis

This affects mainly young birds, and by the time they have reached ten weeks old they are pretty much safe. It is spread by youngsters coming into contact with the droppings of adults, and is caused by a microscopic parasite. It is important to feed chick crumbs treated with a coccidiostat during the first weeks of their lives so that they can gradually build up immunity. This is generally referred to as crumbs with ACS by feed merchants. A liquid coccidiostat is also available to add to drinking water, but can only be bought in large doses, and so is only viable if you are raising a large number of chicks.

The effects of an outbreak are devastating and death is rapid, so take it seriously and take precautions.

Mycoplasma

Most of the UK poultry stocks carry this disease, but it lies dormant within them. If the bird becomes ill or depleted by another ailment, or is severely stressed by transportation or overcrowding, then myco can kick in. A respiratory infection, it causes the birds to cough and sneeze and gape their beaks as they struggle to breathe. Eyes and nostrils may be runny, whilst roosters will stop crowing as their throats are sore. Antibiotics are the only treatment, but they won't completely cure the condition and it can recur at any time if a secondary illness is contracted.

Marek's Disease

We have been lucky enough to avoid this disease, probably at least partly due to our rarely buying in new stock. However, as this is a wind-borne virus that can survive at least a year in the environment, it is fairly common. Commercial stocks are vaccinated within the first 48 hours of their life. Certain breeds, such as Black Rock hybrids, are also vaccinated as a matter of course. They cannot contract the disease, but may still be carriers. Marek's disease is the main reason why I stated earlier in this book that you should not mix vaccinated and unvaccinated poultry.

The disease affects the nervous system and is spread by tiny particles of feather scraps that are infected with the virus being blown from the host bird, and these can travel great distances in strong winds.

Affected birds are eventually struck by paralysis of various parts of their body and flap around pathetically. Although a small percentage survive, they will be carriers of the disease for the rest of their lives and should be culled.

Worms

Like virtually all living things, poultry can be hosts to parasitic worms. Some live in the intestines, but two of the most troublesome live in the crop. Unlike the worms of larger species, those that affect poultry are rarely seen in faeces, the main symptoms being anaemia (pale comb) and loss of appetite and/or weight. A crushed garlic clove in their drinking water is widely believed to be a preventative measure, and it is also claimed that the miraculous diatomaceous earth added to their feed will kill any worms. Whilst there is a good chance either will work, why leave it to chance? It is much better to obtain a traditional medicine from your vet, treat your birds with it every six months, and prevent the problem occurring in the first place.

Most treatments require you to stop eating the eggs for a specified number of days (the withdrawal period), so make sure that you check this out with your vet.

Avian Influenza

Thankfully not something we, or indeed any small poultry keeper in the UK, has experienced yet, but I think it will arrive eventually. By all accounts it seems to be an extremely virulent and fast-acting disease and virtually the first that you will know of it is multiple deaths among your birds, although you may notice the birds' combs and wattles taking on a bluey/purple tinge. If you should suddenly encounter any unexplained deaths among your stock, you should immediately contact your vet and if they have suspicions of AI the authorities will be notified. There is no cure, and because of the highly contagious and pathogenic nature of the disease, any poultry on the premises will be destroyed, as will dangerous contacts and birds on neighbouring premises.

The fear is that the disease will make the jump to humans, possibly by mutating with a human form of influenza. The flu epidemic of 1919 claimed more lives than the First World War, and is now believed to have been caused by a strain of avian influenza. In an attempt to prevent this happening again, UK poultry keepers registered with DEFRA are offered a free flu jab each autumn.

Although AI vaccines for poultry are available, they have not so far been sanctioned by the UK government due to the problem of distinguishing between and identifying vaccinated and unvaccinated stock, as the vaccine appears to show exposure to the virus in subsequent blood tests.

Moulting

Not a problem in itself, as it is a natural event that occurs annually. Sudden shocks or the stress of being moved can also sometimes induce a moult, particularly of the neck feathers, but nothing on the scale of the annual moult, where every feather is dropped in sequence and re-grows. Not all of your flock will moult at the same time, and bantams tend to moult a little earlier than large fowl in my experience. This is good news really, as your birds will stop laying once they have commenced moulting, so a staggered moult means that you may still get a few eggs. If a bird moults and comes back into lay in the autumn you have a good chance of getting some eggs from her throughout the winter, but if she has not recommenced laying by the time the weather changes you can probably say goodbye to any eggs until the spring.

The birds lose their feathers in a set sequence, which starts off gently with head and neck feathers. It becomes most apparent when body and first primaries (the first ten feathers from the wing tip) drop, creating a swathe of feathers in the run. The tail feathers are the next to drop – a rather comical sight – and finally the secondary primaries.

Keep an eye on your birds, and try to identify the ones that moult quickly and with no problems, and come back into lay soon after. These are the birds that you should keep and breed from, discarding any that struggle through their moult. A healthy pullet should complete her moult in eight weeks, and it will take slightly longer in each subsequent year.

You should also take into account hens that have been good mothers, good layers, or those that have been persistently broody.

Autumn is the time to select which birds to keep for next year's laying/breeding programme, and those not selected should either be sold or culled.

The first ten feathers from the wing tip are the primaries, the smaller feathers beyond this are the secondary primaries. New feathers can be seen coming through in the gaps in the wing of this moulting bird.

There are lots of vitamin drinks and cure-alls on the market that claim to make the moult easier, but there seem to be very few facts to back up most of these claims, and the remedies can be expensive. One thing that may be worth trying is apple cider vinegar (ACV) added to the drinking water, as this is widely believed to be beneficial, but it should be the rough-looking cloudy type, not the clear stuff sold in supermarkets for cooking use.

Mice

Mice are a nuisance rather than a menace. At the very least they will increase your costs as they will steal from your chicken's feeders. At worst they can spread disease amongst your stock and cause damage to property. They will feast throughout the night and leave droppings and urinate in your feeders.

As already mentioned, basic measures you can take are to always keep your bulk feed in metal bins and try to hang feeders out of reach.

A couple of strategically placed permanent mousetraps will generally keep the problem under control – it is better to kill any newcomer wandering into your shed than to wait until he has found himself a wife and raised a family. As with all pests, prevention is easier than cure.

Obviously traps should be positioned in areas where your birds, pets or children can't reach them – behind the feed bins is generally a good place. Mouse poisons are available, but we have never found the need to resort to them as traps are generally effective at keeping the numbers down.

Rats

Rats are a menace. They are dangerous, not only to your stock but to you, the keeper, as they carry Weil's Disease. They will attack and kill young birds, dragging them down into their burrows, and will even gnaw the feet and legs of adult birds as they roost. Wooden sheds are no protection against them as they can easily chew their way through the walls or doors.

The danger to humans is through open wounds coming into contact with rat urine. Gloves should be worn at all times when clearing out chicken houses if you suspect the presence of rats. Even handling a water fountain can be hazardous if rats have urinated in the water.

If you are using poison anywhere near livestock it needs to be used responsibly. This means laying the bait inside a box that prevents livestock, pets or children from getting to it. It also needs to be protected against the weather. This box has been set against a wall on a known rat run, and despite the heavy rain it is, as you can see, dry inside.

Our rat problem was solved very quickly, and as our particular bait also kills mice, we now leave the box out at all times.

You have to accept that if you keep poultry, sooner or later the rats will probably find you. The first sign that you are likely to see of them is holes burrowed under your sheds or chicken houses, as these provide a wonderful shelter for their nests.

They are extremely cautious creatures and wary of anything new that appears in their area (especially if they can smell human scent on anything), which makes them quite difficult to deal with. Traps and poisons may be ignored initially. Live traps are probably the safest method to use in close proximity to livestock, as long as you are prepared to dispose of the rats once caught – and I don't mean setting them free away from your property! We have even known the canny pests to tunnel under a wire trap so that the bait drops through and they can steal it without entering the cage.

Rat poison is available, but should be used with caution as a last resort, due to the threat to other wildlife, pets and children if inadvertently left in an area where they can gain access. The safest method is to use a bait box that will both protect the poison from the elements, and non-vermin from the poison.

You can also never account for that little touch twist that we all sometimes call 'Sod's Law'. We found that we had a rat problem so we set a wire cage trap and persevered with it for three weeks. The maize that we used for bait disappeared every night (probably due to mice), but we didn't catch any rats. The rat problem was getting worse, and so we were finally driven to use poison for the first time, investing money that we couldn't afford in a bait box and poison. When I visited the next morning there was a fat rat eyeing me up nervously from within the wire cage trap!

And finally.....

In the Kitchen

I have mentioned earlier that a five or six month old cockerel is in his prime, and this is the time to serve him up for your Sunday dinner.

He will have enjoyed a carefree life, had the warmth of the sun and felt the rain on his back – all things that an intensively farmed chicken won't have had. His varied and natural diet will have produced succulent breast meat that will make your guests green with envy if all they have is the watery pap that the supermarkets sell.

He will also have tough skin. Sorry, but it's a fact of life that a baby's skin is lovely and soft whilst his dad's may be leathery and tough.

Supermarket battery-raised chickens are five or six weeks old and as such are mere babies. Your lad will have had lots of exercise and a comparatively long life, so his skin will be tough. His legs and thighs may be a little tough too, and the meat will be darker and stronger flavoured.

It doesn't present a major problem though; just roast him slowly as you would any chicken, and when he is ready for the table, remove the breast skin before carving. If you find that the leg meat isn't quite to your taste, here are a couple of ideas for an alternative way to serve them:

Chicken Hotpot

An older chicken needs to be cooked long and slow to get it nice and tender. This method works well, and supplies a complete meal in one saucepan. We use a large bantam chicken here, but you can use the tougher legs and thighs from a large fowl equally well.

Ingredients (serves two generously):
One whole small chicken
Flour
2 onions, chopped / 2 carrots, sliced /4oz peas
1 small parsnip, sliced
3 sprays each of parsley and thyme tied in a muslin
2 pints vegetable stock
A little salt and pepper

Skin the chicken and separate the legs and thighs from the body, and also the wings if using them. Remove the breast meat in large pieces. Flour all the pieces well and place them in a large, heavy based saucepan with the onions, carrots and parsnip. Add the parsley and thyme. Cover with the stock and add salt and pepper. Bring to the boil and simmer gently for about 2½ hours. If necessary, thicken with a little flour and water 30 minutes before it is ready, adding the peas 15 minutes later.

Chicken and White Sauce Pie

Ingredients (serves four):
For the pastry:
8oz plain flour
A pinch of salt
2oz margarine
2oz lard
A little milk to glaze the top of the pie.

For the filling:
½ pint milk
1oz butter
1oz plain flour
Salt and pepper
6oz chopped, roasted chicken

Remove the legs and thighs from your roasted chicken. Cut the meat from the bone, discarding any skin and bones. Chop the meat into fairly small pieces.

Prepare the filling by placing the milk, butter and flour in a saucepan and slowly bring them to the boil, stirring constantly until the sauce has thickened. Add the salt and pepper and chopped cooked chicken. Remove them from the heat.

To make the shortcrust pastry, sift the flour and salt into a bowl, add the margarine and lard and rub into the flour with your fingertips until the mixture looks like fine breadcrumbs. Add a little water at a time and press the mix together to form a dough. Place on a lightly floured surface and knead it lightly for a couple of minutes, or until smooth. Roll half of the pastry and use it to line an 8-inch pie dish. Add the chicken mixture, and cover it with the remaining pastry, sealing the edges. Cut some slits in the top and brush the top of the pie with a little milk.

Cook in an oven at 200°C (400°F/Gas mark 6) for 25 minutes until golden brown.

Chicken Curry

Ingredients (serves two generously):
8oz cooked, chopped chicken
1oz butter / 1oz plain flour
1 medium onion, chopped
1 small apple, peeled, cored and chopped
1 tbsp curry powder / ½ tsp ground ginger
½ tsp ground cinnamon
½ pint milk / 5fl oz vegetable stock
1 tablespoon mango chutney / 3oz sultanas

Melt the butter in a large saucepan, add the onion and apple and cook for approximately 5 minutes without browning. Stir in the flour, curry powder and spices and cook for 3 minutes. Gradually stir in the milk and stock, and add the remaining ingredients. Bring to the boil, reduce the heat and simmer for 20 minutes, stirring occasionally. Serve with boiled rice or vegetables of your choice.

A wonderful meal can be made from all the tiny scraps of white meat that remain on your chicken carcass. Here we use the term 'soup' quite loosely, because this nourishing dish is truly a meal in its own right.

Chicken and Vegetable Soup

Ingredients (serves two generously):
4oz chicken leg or thigh meat
2oz chicken breast meat, shredded
2 sticks celery, chopped / 2 onions, chopped
2 carrots, diced / 2oz chopped white cabbage
2 tsp olive oil / 1 tsp tomato puree
1 bay leaf / 1½ pints vegetable stock / 4oz peas
Salt and freshly ground black pepper

Gently fry the celery, onions, cabbage and carrots together with the olive oil for approximately 5 minutes in a large, heavy based saucepan, taking care not to brown them. Liquidise the chicken thigh meat in a blender, together with some of the stock. Add to the saucepan together with the remaining stock, tomato puree, bay leaf and shredded chicken breast and simmer for 20-30 minutes. Add the peas about 5 minutes before serving. Season to taste with salt and pepper. Remove the bay leaf before serving.

The Egg Glut

It happens every year without fail. From around Easter onwards you are inundated with eggs and you get sick of the sight of them! There are only so many eggs that you can eat during the course of a week, and after a while they are viewed in the same light as Christmas turkey, which you seem to be still chewing your way through in early January.

Then in December you rummage in the nest boxes and find them empty for the fifth day in a row and you regret giving away all those eggs back in May.

There are a few ways that you can preserve some of those May eggs to fill the gap during those dark winter months. How about a pickled egg to go with your fish and chips?

Pickled Eggs

12 hard-boiled eggs
1 finely chopped chilli pepper
4 cups of malt vinegar
10 black peppercorns
10 cloves
3 cinnamon sticks
2 tsp allspice

Peel the cold hard-boiled eggs, and place them in a large jar. Bring the vinegar and the spices to the boil in a saucepan and simmer them for 10 minutes. Remove from the heat and cool to about room temperature. Strain the liquid and pour it over the eggs until they are covered. Seal the jar tightly with the lid and store it in a cool, dark place. The longer you keep your pickled eggs, the stronger the flavour becomes.

Preserving Eggs

Eggs used to be preserved whole in isinglass, and huge stoneware crocks were manufactured specifically for the purpose. If you can get isinglass from your pharmacist it is worth having a go. You should only use perfectly clean freshly collected eggs. Do not try this using dirty ones and washing them as you may contaminate the whole batch. Place the eggs point down in your crock or jar, and pour the cooled isinglass over them, completely submerging all the eggs. Seal the jar or cover the crock. Alternatively, the eggs (again fresh, clean and unwashed) can be wiped with liquid paraffin, which seals the shells and prevents contact with the air, which is what causes them to putrefy.

Eggs should easily keep for six months using either method, but it is advisable to break each one into a cup first before adding to your cooking, just in case the shell hasn't been completely sealed. Your nose should tell you the instant you break the shell if there is a problem! They are best used in baking.

Freezing Eggs

Surprisingly, eggs can be frozen, although not whole as the shells will burst and the contents harden. Again, they are only suitable for baking or prepared dishes, but are useful nonetheless.

Lightly beat 5 eggs, and then add either half a teaspoon of sugar (for baking) or salt (for omelets etc.) and pour into a plastic container for freezing.

If you need more specific amounts for recipes you can also follow the above procedure, but freeze the beaten eggs in the compartments of an ice tray. Two and a half tablespoonfuls of the mix will equal one whole egg. Wrap the frozen cubes individually in foil, and store them together in the freezer in a plastic bag. All frozen eggs should be thawed in their storage container at room temperature for one and a half hours.

Contacts & Suppliers

The Battery Hen Welfare Trust
North Parks, Chulmleigh, Devon, EX18 7EJ
www.bhwt.org.uk | 01769 580310

The Humane Slaughter Association
The Old School, Brewhouse Hill, Wheathampstead,
Herts, AL4 8AN
www.hsa.org.uk | 01582 831919

Compassion in World Farming
River Court, Mill Lane, Godalming, Surrey, GU7 1EZ,
www.ciwf.org.uk | 01483 521950

Rare Breeds Survival Trust
Stoneleigh Park, Nr Kenilworth, Warwickshire, CV8 2LG
www.rbst.org.uk | 02476 696551

The Poultry Club,
Keeper's Cottage, 40 Benvarden Road, Dervock, Ballymoney,
Co. Antrim BT53 6NN
www.poultryclub.org | 02820 741056

British Poultry Veterinary Association
7 Mansfield Street, London, W1G 9NQ
www.bvpa.org.uk | 0207 6366541
If your pet is ill and needs treatment, you can find your nearest vet through
the Royal College of Veterinary Surgeons' website - aptly named 'find a
vet'!.Or alternatively, phone them on 0207 2222001.

Verm-X
www.verm-x.com | 0870 8502313
Award-winnnning natural herbal range of liquids and pellets to repel and
control internal parasites in poultry.

Raising Chickens For Eggs and Meat

Brinsea Products Ltd.
Station Road, Sandford, North Somerset, BS25 5RA
www.brinsea.co.uk | 0845 2260120
A wide range of brooding and incubation products.

Ascott Smalholding Supplies Ltd.
Units 9/10, The Old Creamery, Four Crosses, Llanymynech,
SY22 6LP www.ascott.biz | 0845 1306285
Suppliers of everything for the smallholder, from animal feeders, drinkers
and healthcare to incubators and cheese making supplies.

Omlet Ltd.
Tuthill Park, Wardlington, Oxfordshire, OX17 1RR
www.omlet.co.uk | 0845 4502056
Manufacturers of the stylish Eglu chicken house and the Eglu cube
chicken house which come in a number of different colours.
Also providing courses for the novice and new chicken keeper.

Smallholder Supplies
The Old Post Office, 6 Main Street, Branston, Nr. Grantham,
NG32 1RU www.smallholdersupplies.co.uk | 01476 870070
Suppliers of a wide range of smallholder essentials, from feeders, drinkers
and healthcare products to cheese making sundries.

Regency Poultry
Merrydale Farm, Enderby Road, Whetstone, Leicester, LE8 6JL
www.regencypoultry.com | 0116 2866160
Suppliers of poultry accessories, including feeders, drinkers, incubators,
cleaners, disinfectants and healthcare products.

The Domestic Fowl Trust
Station Road, Honeybourne, Evesham, WR11 7QZ
www.domesticfowltrust.co.uk | 01386 833083
A rare breed farm, tea rooms, a children's playground, chicken houses,
poultry supplies and a wide range of 'chicken-related' gifts.

Flyte so Fancy Ltd.

Pulham, Dorchester, Dorset DT2 7DX

www.flytesofancy.co.uk | 01300 345229

Manufacturers and designers of poultry houses, suppliers of poultry accessories and stockists of electric fencing.

Small Holder Range

www.smallholderfeed.co.uk | 01362 822902 |

A complete range of feeds for free range hens including a special feed for rescued battery hens, using no drugs, artificial flavours or yolk pigmenters.

hens4homes

www.hens4homes.co.uk | 01371 878909

Providing hens, complete starter kits and beginners' sessions.

Animal Arks

www.animalarks.co.uk | 01579 382743

Suppliers of traditional redwood poultry housing.

Emvelo

www.emvelo.co.uk | 01494 875848

Providing a range of natural complementary feed supplements, drinking water tonics and housing sprays.

The Great Little Electric Fencing Company

www.snailaway.com | 0845 5616027

Electric poultry netting, scarewires and predator fencing designed to keep your poultry in and predators out.

Forsham Cottage Arks

www.forsham.com | 0800 163797 | (brochures) 01233 820229 (sales)

Designers and builders of poultry and pet housing and also provider of courses for new and prospective chicken owners

www.poultrykeeper.com

The Good Life Press Ltd.
P O Box 536
Preston
PR2 9ZY
01772 652693

The Good Life Press Ltd. publishes a wide range of titles for the smallholder, farmer and country dweller as well as Home Farmer, the monthly magazine for anyone who wants to grab a slice of the good life whether they live in the country or the city.

Other titles of interest:

A Guide to Traditional Pig Keeping by Carol Harris
An Introduction to Keeping Cattle by Peter King
An Introduction to Keeping Sheep by J. Upton/D. Soden
Build It! by Joe Jacobs
Build It!.....Fences and Gates
Build It!...With Pallets by Joe Jacobs
Craft Cider Making by Andrew Lea
First Buy a Field by Rosamund Young
Flowerpot Farming by Jayne Neville
Grow and Cook by Brian Tucker
How to Butcher Livestock and Game by Paul Peacock
Making Jams and Preserves by Diana Sutton
No Time to Grow by Tim Wootton
Precycle! by Paul Peacock
Talking Sheepdogs by Derek Scrimgeour
The Bread and Butter Book by Diana Sutton
The Cheese Making Book by Paul Peacock
The Frugal Life by Piper Terrett
The Pocket Guide to Wild Food by Paul Peacock
The Polytunnel Companion by Jayne Neville
The Sausage Book by Paul Peacock
The Shepherd's Pup (DVD) with Derek Scrimgeour
Showing Sheep by Sue Kendrick
The Smoking and Curing Book by Paul Peacock
The Urban Farmer's Handbook by Paul Peacock
A Cut Above the Rest (a butchering DVD)

www.goodlifepress.co.uk
www.homefarmer.co.uk